Also by Harry Lampert
The Fun Way to Serious Bridge
Declarer Play and Opening Leads

THE FUN WAY TO ADVANCED BRIDGE

By
Harry Lampert

Published by
Devyn Press, Inc.
Louisville, Kentucky

Copyright © 1985, 1990 by Harry Lampert

All rights reserved. No part of this
book may be reproduced in any form
without the permission of Devyn Press.

Printed in the United States of America.

Devyn Press, Inc.
3600 Chamberlain Lane, Suite 230
Louisville, KY 40241
1-800-274-2221

ISBN 0-910791-77-5

To our grandson,
Michael,
whose birth
and
the birth of the idea
for this book
arrived
at the same time

CONTENTS

INTRODUCTION

Here we go again! Many of you are at the crossroads. You can remain at the same level or take a giant leap into the world of playing better bridge.

You've presumably read *The Fun Way to Serious Bridge*, and/or taken courses at the local bridge club or at adult ed. You've played with friends and neighbors, some better . . . some worse. Now, you'd like to make the breakthrough and become a really good bridge player.

How do you do it? Does the answer lie in a proliferation of conventions, with more things to remember, and more things to *forget*? Or does the solution lie in learning and understanding the "little" things that make life easier at the bridge table?

The hints contained in this book can easily be learned by the average player. The beneficial results are fully attainable by the same average player . . . and before you realize it, you are no longer just an average player!

You will probably be amazed by how supposedly complex concepts can become so simple. With conscientious application, you can surprise yourself and your friends with the gigantic improvement in your game . . . and at the same time you'll have a lot of fun doing it.

Of course, we'll give you insights into some important conventional bids as well. You'll use only those you and your partners are comfortable with, and you'll have a working knowledge of others if your opponents use them.

The delicate nuances of defensive play, with emphasis on partnership communications—declarer play, planning and techniques, bidding methods and good judgment—will all be highlighted.

And, most important, take advantage of our "For Cryin' Out Loud" practice sessions, which we'll discuss fully later on. They'll truly put you into a new league. You'll notice the improvement and have fun at the same time.

So here it is, *The Fun Way to Advanced Bridge*. Go to it!

DEFENSIVE PLAY

If you are at all like my friends, you are never dealt more than five high-card points per hand. That means you're going to be a defender much more often than you are declarer.

But even if you are one of those rare birds who get their fair share of high cards, statistically you're twice as likely to be a defender than a declarer.

So if you're going to be defending most of the time, good defense becomes an enormous factor that leads to winning bridge.

The big problem in defense is that you don't see your partner's cards and he doesn't see yours. Your card play, therefore, must not only be *effective*, but must also *send* vital information to your partner.

One of the most important keys to successful defense is the opening lead. Your opening shot is based on only the thirteen cards you see and clues gathered from the bidding.

Once you've led, you can't say, "Oops, sorry!" upon seeing the dummy.

A sensible approach in deciding what to lead is to establish your strategy. Then, which suit to lead and which card to lead fall into place.

First, review the bidding (or lack of bidding) that has taken place. It may furnish a valuable clue to the road your defense should take.

Notrump Opening Leads

Notrump bidding is often quite revealing as to the high card strength of the opponents *and your partner*.

Simple arithmetic usually does the trick. With standard bidding, for instance, if the opponents' bidding has gone, "1 NT," "2 NT," "3 NT," you know that their combined holding is 26 points (within one point, more or less).

Here are some examples:

BIDDING:		TOTAL POINTS
opp't	*opp't's partner*	
1 NT = 16–18 pts. 3 NT = 17–18 pts.	2 NT = 8–9 pts.	26 pts. (±)
1 NT = 16–18 pts. PASS = 16 pts.	2 NT = 8–9 pts.	24 or 25 pts.
Or even if there's a Stayman sequence:		
opp't	*opp't's partner*	
1 NT = 16–18 pts. 2 ♦ = no major REBID: PASS = 16 pts.	2 ♣ = Got a major? 2 NT = 8–9 pts. max.	24 or 25 pts.
or REBID: 3 NT = 17–18 pts.		26 pts. (±)

Or if a sequence starts with a suit bid:		
opp't	*opp't's partner*	
1 ♠ = 13+ pts. REBID: PASS = 13–15 pts.	1 NT = 6–9 pts.	19–24 pts.
or REBID: 2 NT = 17–18 pts.	PASS = 6–7 pts.	24 pts. (±)
or REBID: 2 NT = 17–18 pts.	3 NT = 8–9 pts.	26 pts. (±)
or REBID: 3 NT = 19+ pts.	PASS = 6–9 pts.	25–28 pts.

Now that you "know" the opponents' point count, it's easy to figure out how strong your partner's hand is. Add your point count to the opponents' point count and then subtract the total from 40 points. That will give you your partner's point count.

Example:

Opponents combined points:	26
Plus your points:	6
Equal:	32
Subtract from:	40
Partner's point count:	8

If you like fancy formulas, here's one:

40 POINTS − [OPPTS. POINTS + YOUR POINTS] = PARTNER'S POINTS

If you've done your simple arithmetic, you now know your side has basically one of three types of defensive strength combinations.

1. The partnership strength is fairly equally distributed.
2. You hold the preponderance of the strength.
3. Your partner has the preponderance of the strength.

1. PARTNERSHIP STRENGTH EQUALLY DISTRIBUTED

Under these circumstances leading your best suit can work out quite well. Use standard leads that will communicate with your partner: top of a sequence, top of an interior sequence, or ("fourth best") fourth card down.

Examples: Leading against 3 NT contract

♠ 8 6 3	♠ A J 10 8 7	♠ 9 8
♥ K 7	♥ 10 6 3	♥ A Q 9 3 2
♦ K 8 2	♦ K 4 2	♦ 10 8 7
♣ Q J 10 7 6	♣ 9 7	♣ J 9 7
Lead: ♣ queen	Lead: ♠ jack	Lead: ♥ three

2. YOU HAVE THE PREPONDERANCE OF THE STRENGTH

There are some hands where partner's strength is virtually nil.

If you've kept your big mouth shut during the auction, this is something *you* know that declarer doesn't. Unless you have a long suit or a sound sequence (like K Q J X or Q J 10 X), leading from strength will often cost you tricks.

Make a passive lead from your weak suit. You won't be giving up a thing. You won't be fooling your partner either. The chance of his taking the lead is almost nonexistent.

Examples: Leading against 3 NT contract

♠ 9 7 2	♠ A Q	♠ A Q 4
♥ A Q 3	♥ 7 6 3 2	♥ A J 10
♦ K J 10 4	♦ K J 10 6	♦ 9 6 3
♣ K J 3	♣ K J 8	♣ Q 10 9 3
Lead: ♠ two	Lead: ♥ two	Lead: ♦ three

3. PARTNER HAS THE PREPONDERANCE OF STRENGTH

If you have no entries, try to figure out partner's best suit, and lead that suit. Careful attention to the opponents' bidding may indicate which suit to lead. If partner has been listening as well as you, he will know you have very little strength.

Important: If there is a choice of suits, choosing the major suit is usually wiser.

Examples: Leading against 3 NT contract

A. ♠ 9 8 2	B. ♠ 8 6 3	C. ♠ 9 3
♥ 7 6 5	♥ 10 9	♥ 10 6 3
♦ 10 7 6 3	♦ 9 6 3 2	♦ 10 7 6 2
♣ 9 3 2	♣ J 5 3 2	♣ 9 8 4 3

Holding these hands, you are on lead after the following standard bidding by the opponents:

A. 1 NT 2 NT	B. 1 NT 3 NT	C. 1 NT 2 ♣
3 NT Pass	Pass	2 ♦ 3 ♥
		3 NT Pass
Lead: ♠ nine	Lead: ♥ ten	Lead: ♠ nine

In each case, because you hold a very poor hand, you try to find partner's best suit.

HAND A. Your spade holding is slightly better than your hearts. The spade nine may bolster partner's suit.

HAND B. The opponents have not attempted to reach a major suit contract. Your heart ten may help solidify your partner's holding in that suit. He probably has five hearts, maybe six.

HAND C. The bidding almost guarantees that your partner holds at least four spades. The spade lead may very well hit partner's best suit.

These are all ideas for you to consider when you make opening leads against no trump contracts. However, there is no substitute for listening to the bidding and *thinking at the table.*

Opening Leads Against Suit Contracts

Here are four of the prevailing strategies in use when defending against suit contracts. Decide which one fits the hand you're holding, and this will usually determine which suit to play and which card to lead.

1. SET UP HIGH CARDS

This is the most common defensive ploy. Leading the top of a sequence often sets up the card or cards below it as potential winning tricks.

Leading the king from king, queen, jack, may promote the queen, and possibly the jack, too, as winners.

Leading an ace, however, unless it is partner's suit, quite often sets up the king, queen, etc. (and sometimes the complete suit) as tricks for the declarer.

EXAMPLE:

North
♠ J 8 6 4 2
♥ 8 5 2
♦ J 5
♣ A J 9

West
♠ K 7
♥ K Q 10 9 6
♦ A 2
♣ K 10 6 3

East
♠ 5
♥ J 4
♦ 9 8 6 4 3
♣ Q 8 5 4 2

South
♠ A Q 10 9 3
♥ A 7 3
♦ K Q 10 7
♣ 7

BIDDING:

North	East	South	West
Pass	Pass	1♠	2♥
2♠	Pass	4♠	Pass
Pass	Pass		

OPENING LEAD: ♥king

To defeat the optimistic four spade contract, the lead of the ♥king is essential. After declarer wins his ace, he must eventually relinquish the lead to West, permitting him to garner two heart tricks plus the trump king and diamond ace.

Any other lead permits declarer to set up a diamond trick for a heart discard from dummy. The opening lead of the ♦ace and a diamond continuation in the phantom hope for a ruff, will, as a matter of fact, enable declarer to make an overtrick.

2. CUT DOWN RUFFS

When you have reason to believe that you or partner have good control of the side suits, leading trumps may prevent some of your side's high cards from being ruffed by dummy and/or declarer. Upon gaining the lead subsequently, you can continue the same strategy by leading trumps again.

Listening to the bidding often reveals when this tactic will be effective.

A denial of support in the side suits and an eventual agreement on the trump suit by the declaring side may signal the advisability of leading trumps.

A word of caution: Be sure that the opponents do not hold an easy-to-establish, runnable side suit. Your lead of a trump might then backfire.

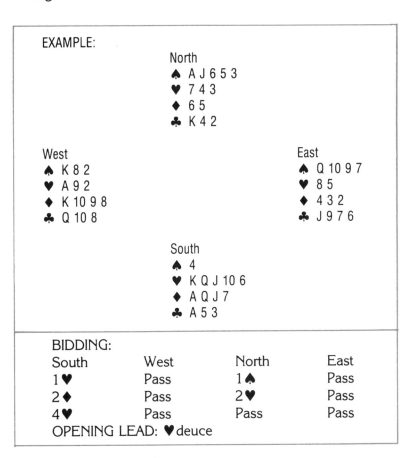

EXAMPLE:

North
♠ A J 6 5 3
♥ 7 4 3
♦ 6 5
♣ K 4 2

West
♠ K 8 2
♥ A 9 2
♦ K 10 9 8
♣ Q 10 8

East
♠ Q 10 9 7
♥ 8 5
♦ 4 3 2
♣ J 9 7 6

South
♠ 4
♥ K Q J 10 6
♦ A Q J 7
♣ A 5 3

BIDDING:

South	West	North	East
1♥	Pass	1♠	Pass
2♦	Pass	2♥	Pass
4♥	Pass	Pass	Pass

OPENING LEAD: ♥ deuce

The bidding indicates that dummy may be short in diamonds. You want to reduce the possibility of your diamond winners being ruffed in dummy.

The lead of a small trump permits you to maintain control of the suit. When you next obtain the lead, the continuation of the ace and another trump effectively prevents declarer from ruffing a diamond in dummy. This holds the declarer to nine tricks.

3. GIVE YOURSELF (OR PARTNER) A RUFF

Leading from shortness in your partner's known or implied suit is frequently a safe and effective lead. It will set up high cards for your partner and has the potential of establishing ruffs for yourself. A singleton or a doubleton is a sound lead in these circumstances.

However, leading a singleton in the opponents' suit in the hope of obtaining a ruff is quite a different matter. You could very well be setting up their entire suit.

A good principle to use is: Do not lead a singleton in the opponents' side suit unless you hold first or second round control of the trump suit, *and* have a way of reaching partner so that he can return the suit you led for a ruff.

In the following example the singleton lead in declarer's side suit is the only lead that defeats the contract. All the conditions are prevalent for the successful use of this tactic: first round control of the trump suit, plus a way of reaching partner in his suit.

EXAMPLE:

```
                        North
                        ♠ J 7 5 4
                        ♥ J 6
                        ♦ A J 10 7
                        ♣ J 10 9

West                                          East
♠ A 6 3                                       ♠ 2
♥ K 10 5 3                                    ♥ A Q 9 8 4 2
♦ 8                                           ♦ 5 3 2
♣ 7 5 4 3 2                                   ♣ K Q 6

                        South
                        ♠ K Q 10 9 8
                        ♥ 7
                        ♦ K Q 9 6 4
                        ♣ A 8
```

EAST-WEST: Vulnerable

BIDDING:

South	West	North	East
1 ♠	Pass	2 ♠	3 ♥
4 ♦	Pass	4 ♠	Pass
Pass	Pass		

OPENING LEAD: ♦ eight

Declarer wins your opening lead and then leads a trump. You can win the first trump lead and return a heart or, better yet, hold off for one round, permitting partner to signal on the next trump lead with the nine of hearts.

You now return a heart to partner's ace and he gives you a diamond ruff. Eventually partner has to get a club trick, which sets the contract.

When can you give partner a ruff? The clues are often right there, in the bidding. All you have to do is listen. The clues are frequently clear-cut.

One possibility is: The opponents along the way have bid and supported a side suit, indicating an eight-card fit. You hold four cards to the ace in that suit. Your lead of the ace and another will give your partner a ruff without costing you a trick. Or, if you hold five cards (no ace) in the suit, bingo! Partner will ruff the opening lead.

Also, if you hold four cards in the side suit, plus the trump ace, you may lead the suit. When you get the lead again with the trump ace, you can then give partner his ruff. *CAUTION:* Make sure that your trump holding does not exceed two cards. You should feel sure that partner has at least two trumps for your maneuver to be effective.

EXAMPLE:

North
♠ A 10 9
♥ Q J 9
♦ K Q 9 6
♣ Q 10 7

West
♠ J 8 6 4 2
♥ A 6
♦ A 8 5 2
♣ 9 3

East
♠ K Q 5 3
♥ 4 3 2
♦ 3
♣ K 8 5 4 2

South
♠ 7
♥ K 10 8 7 5
♦ J 10 7 4
♣ A J 6

BIDDING:

North	East	South	West
1 ♦	Pass	1 ♥	Pass
1 NT	Pass	2 ♦	Pass
2 ♥	Pass	3 ♥	Pass
4 ♥	Pass	Pass	Pass

OPENING LEAD: ♦ ace

The double-barreled power of the four diamonds headed by the ace, plus the trump ace, enabled East-West to defeat this otherwise sound contract.

The ♦ ace lead and diamond continuation permitted East to obtain his first ruff. Upon obtaining the lead again with the trump ace, West was able to lead another diamond for his partner to ruff.

SHORTEN DECLARER'S TRUMPS TO FEWER THAN YOURS.

4. FORCE DECLARER TO RUFF

When you hold four or more trumps, or have reason to believe partner has such a holding, forcing declarer to ruff is usually a sound strategy.

Leading your side's long and strong suit is the way to do it. Continue to do so at every opportunity. After declarer has ruffed two or more times, he may wind up having fewer trumps than you do. Now, *you* become master of the hand.

In the example on the following page, an opening lead of partner's diamond suit sets the stage for defeat of the sound four heart contract. Continued diamond returns whenever East gets the lead, plus careful play in the side suits, eventually destroy declarer's control of the trump suit.

EXAMPLE:

North
- ♠ K 10 7
- ♥ K 9 5
- ♦ 9 6 4 3
- ♣ J 9 5

West
- ♠ 8 5 3 2
- ♥ 2
- ♦ K 8 2
- ♣ 10 6 4 3 2

East
- ♠ 6 4
- ♥ Q 10 8 6
- ♦ A Q J 10 5
- ♣ A 7

South
- ♠ A Q J 9
- ♥ A J 7 4 3
- ♦ 7
- ♣ K Q 8

NORTH-SOUTH: Vulnerable

BIDDING:

South	West	North	East
1 ♥	Pass	2 ♥	3 ♦
4 ♥	Pass	Pass	Pass

OPENING LEAD: ♦ two

HELP YOUR PARTNER

The best way to counteract declarer's advantage of knowing *all* his assets, while you know only *half* your side's cards, is for you and partner to help each other as much as possible.

You have a number of weapons at your command. Attitude signals, count signals and suit preference signals top the list.

True, they often are revealing to the declarer as well, but getting the information to partner has priority. In most cases, declarer can do nothing at all about it. In any event, declarer already knows all your side's assets. He may or may not know how they are distributed.

If you can help partner make the proper decisions, you are well ahead of the game.

Let's review briefly standard defensive signaling.

Signaling

1. **ATTITUDE**

   When partner leads a high card, if you want him to continue the suit, play high-low; if you want him to discontinue it, or you have no interest, play up-the-line (low-high). Likewise, when you cannot follow suit and have to discard, discard high-low in suits that interest you and low-high (up-the-line) in those suits where you have no interest.

2. **COUNT**

   Show an even number of cards in a suit by playing high-low; an odd number of cards by playing up-the-line, low to high. This is particularly helpful when declarer is playing a suit and partner wants to know when to take a trick in that suit. It also enables partner to count declarer's hand.

3. **SUIT PREFERENCE**

   Quite often partner has a choice of two suits to lead. You indicate a preference between the two suits by signaling in a third suit. Play the highest card you can spare in the third suit for the higher ranking suit, play your lowest card in the third suit for the lower ranking suit.

4. **TRUMP SIGNALING**

   Count signaling in the trump suit is the opposite of normal count signals. With two cards, play low-high. With three cards, play high-low.

All signals are designed to help partner make the correct decision. You sometimes have to improvise to achieve the best defense.

Here's a little "Go-Stop" signal:

The opponents are in a suit contract, and partner leads the king of a side suit. This is dummy's and your holding in the suit led:

DUMMY	
Q 5	
	YOU
	J 8 6 2

You would like partner to *continue*, so you play the six. Partner then plays the ace. You now want him to *stop!* You therefore play the eight (up-the-line).

Let us see what might have happened had you played differently.

If you had played the deuce on the first round, partner might not have continued the suit. Perhaps declarer could discard the queen from dummy later.

Or if, having first played the six, you had next played the deuce, partner might have led a third round, possibly giving declarer a ruff and a sluff.

Another Helpful Hint: *Never expect partner to do something that you can do yourself.*

Suppose you are faced with this situation:

The opponents are in a four heart contract and your side competed along the way, partner having bid spades.

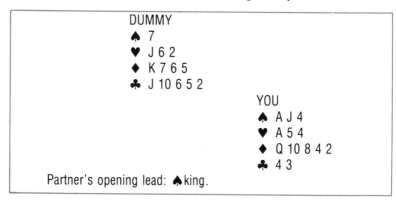

DUMMY
♠ 7
♥ J 6 2
♦ K 7 6 5
♣ J 10 6 5 2

YOU
♠ A J 4
♥ A 5 4
♦ Q 10 8 4 2
♣ 4 3

Partner's opening lead: ♠ king.

From your hand it is "obvious" that partner should switch to a trump. You could play the "discouraging" ♠4 and partner *might* switch to a trump. But he could possibly also switch to a club, or even a diamond.

Take partner off the hook! Overtake the ♠king with the ace! Now play the ace and a small trump. No matter how declarer wriggles he cannot make the contract.

Here is the complete hand, and let's see what would have happened if your side had not shifted to a trump:

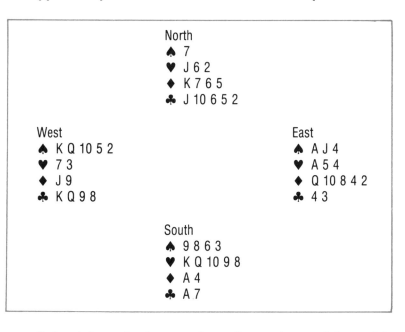

North
♠ 7
♥ J 6 2
♦ K 7 6 5
♣ J 10 6 5 2

West
♠ K Q 10 5 2
♥ 7 3
♦ J 9
♣ K Q 9 8

East
♠ A J 4
♥ A 5 4
♦ Q 10 8 4 2
♣ 4 3

South
♠ 9 8 6 3
♥ K Q 10 9 8
♦ A 4
♣ A 7

If the defense leads a spade, a diamond or a club at trick two, declarer easily makes the contract by trumping three spades in dummy. If your mission in life is to bawl out partner, allow him to guess what to do at trick two. In this case, he has at least three ways to go wrong. But if your aim is to be a winner, adopt a philosophy of "I'd rather do it myself, partner!"

WHEN TO BREAK THE RULES

There are standard opening leads that we all know. Every once in a while, circumstances require a deviation from the normal procedures.

Usually, when holding three or four cards headed by a single honor (other than an ace), the proper opening lead is a low card.

However, there are some situations when it is wise to lead the honor:

1. When you want to retain the lead, so that you can make the next play through dummy.

2. When you have reason to believe that dummy has a key honor in the suit and you want to immediately attack that honor.

Careful attention to the bidding will often help you to the correct use of these variations from the norm.

Here are two examples:

You are West and your partner is the dealer. Your side is vulnerable, the opponents are not, and you hold these cards:

♠ 6 5   ♥ K 7 5 2   ♦ Q J 5 3 2   ♣ 9 8

The bidding proceeds:

East	South	West	North
1 ♥	1 ♠	2 ♥	2 ♠
3 ♥	4 ♠	Pass	Pass
Pass			

It's your lead and it certainly makes sense to lead partner's suit. Normally, you would play the ♥ deuce. But judging from the bidding, the suit will not survive a second round without being ruffed. Therefore, play the ♥ king so that you can retain the lead and, if necessary, attack a key card in dummy.

Here is the dummy you see:

♠ K J 3 2
♥ 9 8 6
♦ K 9 8
♣ 10 4 3

On your ♥ king, partner plays the queen and declarer the ten.

It is obvious that declarer has no more hearts. You had four of them, dummy three and partner had five. Declarer's ♥ 10 must be a singleton and you are in position to switch suits. Partner has helped you by playing the ♥ queen, a suit preference signal to switch to diamonds rather than clubs. You now play the ♦ queen, covered by dummy's king and partner's ace. A diamond is returned to your jack and declarer cannot avoid losing a club trick to the ace, for a one-trick set.

Here is the entire hand:

```
                    North
                    ♠ K J 3 2
                    ♥ 9 8 6
                    ♦ K 9 8
                    ♣ 10 4 3

West                                    East
♠ 6 5                                   ♠ 9 7
♥ K 7 5 2                               ♥ A Q J 4 3
♦ Q J 5 3 2                             ♦ A 10 6
♣ 9 8                                   ♣ A 7 2

                    South
                    ♠ A Q 10 8 4
                    ♥ 10
                    ♦ 7 4
                    ♣ K Q J 6 5
```

Notice what would have happened if you had made the standard lead of the ♥2. Partner would have won the trick but would have found himself unable to lead a diamond without conceding a trick to the ♦king. Declarer would ruff the heart return, draw trumps and then play clubs until East wins it. He would now trump the heart return and discard two diamonds on the set up clubs. He would wind up losing one trick in each of the three side suits, making his four spade contract.

Another instance when it is wise to lead an honor in partner's bid suit, rather than a small card, is when the bidding strongly indicates that dummy has an honor in that suit.

This is particularly true when dummy has bid notrump, either as an opening bid, or along the way despite your partner's bid of that suit.

Here is an example:

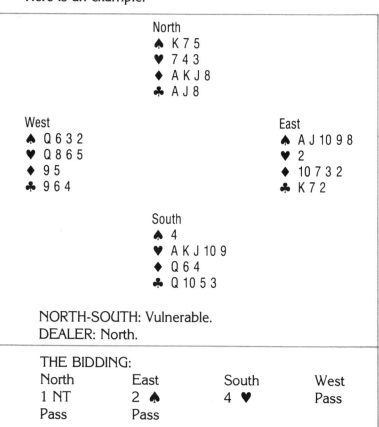

North
♠ K 7 5
♥ 7 4 3
♦ A K J 8
♣ A J 8

West
♠ Q 6 3 2
♥ Q 8 6 5
♦ 9 5
♣ 9 6 4

East
♠ A J 10 9 8
♥ 2
♦ 10 7 3 2
♣ K 7 2

South
♠ 4
♥ A K J 10 9
♦ Q 6 4
♣ Q 10 5 3

NORTH-SOUTH: Vulnerable.
DEALER: North.

THE BIDDING:

North	East	South	West
1 NT	2 ♠	4 ♥	Pass
Pass	Pass		

West is on lead and he decides to lead partner's suit. Let's see what happens if he makes the standard lead of the ♠ two. North plays the five and East wins with the eight.

East cannot return the ♠ ace without setting up the ♠ king in dummy. So let's say he returns a low diamond. South wins and tries a club finesse, which loses, and East leads another diamond, dummy winning. Declarer takes the trump finesse, losing to West. South ruffs the spade return, draws trumps and so makes the contract.

But now look how much better life becomes if your opening lead is the ♠ queen. If North ducks, you continue the suit, forcing declarer to ruff.

At this point, declarer has two roads to take.

1. South may decide to take the club finesse which loses to East. Another spade comes back and declarer has to ruff again. He now has *fewer trumps* than West and this is the situation:

```
                    North
                    ♠ —
                    ♥ 7 4 3
                    ♦ A K J 8
                    ♣ A J

West                                        East
♠ 6                                         ♠ J 10
♥ Q 8 6 5                                   ♥ 2
♦ 9 5                                       ♦ 10 7 3 2
♣ 9 6                                       ♣ 7 2

                    South
                    ♠ —
                    ♥ A K J
                    ♦ Q 6 4
                    ♣ Q 5 3
```

Declarer may now take the ace of trumps and lead two rounds of diamonds. He next plays the ace, queen, and another club, which you ruff with the eight of trumps. You exit with a spade and score your ♥ queen at the end for the setting trick.

2. If declarer took the other road, he would cash the trump king, enter dummy with a diamond and take the trump finesse. You win with the queen and return a spade which declarer has to ruff, leaving this situation:

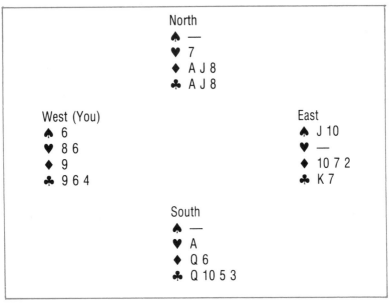

North
♠ —
♥ 7
♦ A J 8
♣ A J 8

West (You)
♠ 6
♥ 8 6
♦ 9
♣ 9 6 4

East
♠ J 10
♥ —
♦ 10 7 2
♣ K 7

South
♠ —
♥ A
♦ Q 6
♣ Q 10 5 3

No matter what declarer does, there is no way he can avoid losing a trick to your ♥ eight and a trick to your partner's ♣ king.

The nonstandard opening lead thus defeats a contract that would have succeeded with the standard opening lead.

Another occasional deviation from standard opening lead practice is available when you have supported partner's suit and hold three or four little cards. Leading the top card will not fool partner, but will tell him that you do not hold an honor card in the suit. He can then figure out the appropriate play. He knows you do not hold a doubleton because you previously raised him in that suit.

ACTIVE DEFENSE OR PASSIVE DEFENSE

When to try to establish and cash tricks quickly and when to lie back and wait for declarer to make the first move in a given suit are important decisions facing thinking defenders.

ACTIVE DEFENSE

When you know declarer has a long suit available for discards, it is important to cash your winners before declarer can accomplish his mission.

As a preventive measure, it is therefore sometimes necessary to make a risky play that you would not make under ordinary circumstances:

EXAMPLE:

Dummy
♠ A 7 6 5
♥ Q 8 6
♦ A K Q 9 4
♣ 8

You
♠ 8 4
♥ K J 10
♦ J 10 2
♣ A K 9 7 3

You lead the ♣king against a four spade contract and see dummy's magnificent diamonds staring you in the face. You know that unless your side can collect some heart tricks quickly, declarer will be able to discard his heart losers on dummy's diamonds. So you make the risky play of the ♥ king, hoping partner has the ace. If he has it, you continue with the jack and hope to wind up with three heart tricks.

Leading the ♥ jack might have proved just as effective, but it could give partner a chance to go wrong. If declarer did not cover the jack with dummy's queen, partner might hop up with the ace, not knowing for sure who held the king. Whenever possible, avoid giving partner a guess.

Here is the entire hand:

```
                        Dummy
                        ♠ A 7 6 5
                        ♥ Q 8 6
                        ♦ A K Q 9 4
                        ♣ 8

    You                                     Partner
    ♠ 8 4                                   ♠ J
    ♥ K J 10                                ♥ A 7 5 4
    ♦ J 10 2                                ♦ 6 5 3
    ♣ A K 9 7 3                             ♣ 10 6 5 4 2

                        Declarer
                        ♠ K Q 10 9 3 2
                        ♥ 9 3 2
                        ♦ 8 7
                        ♣ Q J
```

PASSIVE DEFENSE

There are some combinations of cards which penalize the side that first leads that suit. In these cases, adopt a *passive* role in that suit. When it is your turn to lead, play a different suit, one in which you permit declarer to win tricks he would ordinarily win in any event. Then let him do the leading in situations such as:

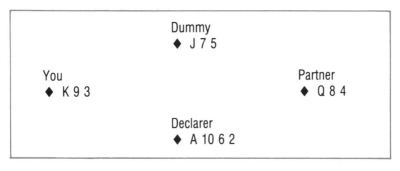

If dummy or declarer leads the suit first, they cannot avoid losing two tricks to your side.

But if you or partner leads the suit first, declarer can hold you to one trick.

WHICH CARD SHOULD I SAVE?

When that nasty ol' declarer starts running a long suit against you, you often have to decide which cards to save and which to discard. Cooperation with your partner will often supply the answers. Here's how he can help:

1. **COUNT SIGNALS** in suits declarer is leading can help determine how many cards declarer has in those suits. Partner plays high-low to show that he holds an even number of cards in the suit, and low-high to show an odd number of cards. By simple arithmetic you can often figure out how many cards declarer holds in those suits.

2. **INFORMATIVE DISCARDS**—high-low signals in suits in which he has strength, up-the-line signals (low to high) in suits he does not control. Sometimes partner cannot afford to discard high cards in a suit he is interested in. In that case, he discards *low cards* in the suits in which he is *not* interested. By negative inference, he is suggesting strength or interest in the suit in which he has made no discards.

Incidentally, while partner is busy helping you, I hope *you* are helping *your* partner, too!

REMEMBER THE BIDDING

With careful attention to the bidding you can often get a good count of the hand. Knowing how many cards declarer has in each suit will often help you decide which cards to save.

A good rule of thumb is to retain as many cards as dummy has in a suit (if the dummy is reachable) and/or to keep as many cards as declarer has in a suit.

Even if your holding is as low as 9 4 3 2, it may be advisable to hold on to that suit if you know declarer has four cards of the suit.

```
EXAMPLE:
                    Dummy
                    J 7 5

Partner                          You
Q 10                             9 4 3 2
                    Declarer
                    A K 8 6
```

If partner holds Q 10, your nine becomes a fourth-round winner.

There are other little signs to look for that may help you decide which cards to save.

In a suit contract, if declarer did not ruff a loser in dummy when he could have done so, he most likely doesn't have a loser in that suit. You can therefore safely discard your high cards in that suit.

Counting the declarer's high-card points, and relating them to the bidding, is another guide to what to hold or discard.

If declarer had opened the bidding with one notrump, and has shown up with 13 points so far, and you are wondering who has the missing king, you can be pretty sure that the declarer has it.

If declarer, responding to partner's opening of one in a major suit, has bid a nonforcing one notrump and has already shown up with 8 or 9 points, you can safely assume that *your partner* has any missing king or ace.

Counting and signaling are good guides to *"which card should I save."*

WHICH CARD SHOULD I RETURN?

Partner has led a suit, you have won the trick and want to return that suit. Which card do you return?

It is often important for partner to know how many cards you originally held in the suit.

A. With an original holding of four cards, return the lowest.
B. With an original holding of three cards, return the highest.

Here's why:

(In these examples, partner has led the three against a no-trump contract.)

A.		
	Dummy 7 5	
Partner K J 9 3		You A 8 6 2
	Declarer Q 10 4	

```
B.                          Dummy
                            7 5


        Partner                                     You
        K J 9 3                                     A 8 2
                            Declarer
                            Q 10 6 4
```

EXAMPLE A:

After winning the ace, you return the deuce, indicating you originally held four cards. Declarer plays the ten and partner wins with the jack. Since your partner knows you started with four cards in the suit, that leaves only three for declarer. Your partner can therefore safely cash the king, felling declarer's queen, and win the fourth trick as well.

EXAMPLE B:

After winning the ace, you return the eight this time, thus denying an original holding of four cards. Again declarer covers with the ten and partner wins with the jack. But now he knows declarer originally held four cards. He therefore does not cash the king because it would surely make declarer's queen a trick. Knowing this, partner switches to another suit, hoping to reach your hand so that you can lead the original suit again through the declarer.

Like everything else in bridge, judgment plays a key role. If you hold four cards such as A J 10 2, it makes more sense, after winning the ace, to lead back the jack instead of the deuce. This guarantees trapping declarer's possible Q 9 4. It also unblocks the suit if partner started with A 9 X X X of the suit.

THE UPPERCUT

Every once in a while, when you are a defender, a presumably useless trump can become a very powerful weapon through the use of a maneuver delightfully nicknamed "the uppercut."

Let's look at the example on the following page.

The opponents are in four spades and your partner is on lead.

Partner leads the ♥ king, followed by the ace, and you high-low with the ♥ nine and two. A third heart is now led to dummy's queen. Here is your chance to be a hero. *Give 'em the uppercut!* Trump with the ♠ eight (not the deuce)!

Let's see what happens. Your ♠ eight forces declarer to overtrump with the ♠ queen. This establishes a sure trump trick for your partner's ♠ J 10 3, and declarer also has no way to avoid a diamond loser. The uppercut defeats an otherwise sound contract.

Dummy
♠ A 9 7
♥ Q 7 5
♦ 8 7 6 5
♣ Q J 10

Partner
♠ J 10 3
♥ A K J 10 8 3
♦ 4 3
♣ 9 7

You
♠ 8 2
♥ 9 2
♦ A 10 9 2
♣ 8 6 5 3 2

Declarer
♠ K Q 6 5 4
♥ 6 4
♦ K Q J
♣ A K 4

Notice what would have happened if you had incorrectly trumped with the ♠ two. Declarer would have overtrumped with the ♠ four, drawn trumps, surrendered a diamond trick and made his contract.

Keep your eyes open for the uppercut. It comes up in actual play more often than you may think.

YESSIR! THAT'S MY QUEEN!

WHEN YOU'VE GOT IT . . . FLAUNT IT!

If you know declarer knows you've got it, play the card declarer knows you have as soon as it is safe to do so.

Here's an example:

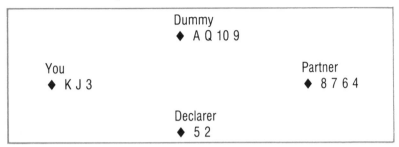

Dummy
♦ A Q 10 9

You
♦ K J 3

Partner
♦ 8 7 6 4

Declarer
♦ 5 2

Declarer is playing this side suit in a trump contract. He leads from his hand and finesses the queen. He next plays the ace. You should play the king—the card declarer knows you possess. Declarer may now try to take a ruffing finesse against partner's supposed jack. If he does, you will score your jack.

If you had played the jack instead of the king, declarer could not go wrong. He would know that you still have the king. He would ruff the nine, felling your king and establishing the ten as a trick.

Here's another example:

Dummy
A J 7

You
Q 10 6

Partner
8 4 2

Declarer
K 9 5 3

Declarer leads the three and finesses the jack. On the ace lead you should play the queen. Declarer may now finesse partner for the ten, giving you a trick instead. (Incidentally, partner may create an illusion by giving a fake count signal. By playing the four and then the deuce, he might persuade a watchful declarer that he originally held four cards.)

Whenever you hold cards of equal value, remember, play the cards declarer *knows* you have as soon as you can.

DECLARER PLAY

DON'T LET ANYBODY ELSE PLAY THE DUMMY, NOT EVEN THE DUMMY!

Don't permit partner or *anyone else* to play any card from dummy . . . even if it is a singleton!

You need the extra time to decide which card to play from your hand *before* it is your turn to play.

Here is a possible situation: You are in a notrump contract and the ♠king has been led.

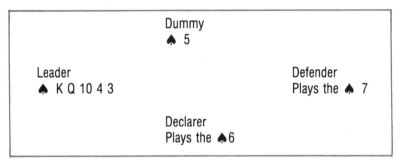

From the leader's point of view, he may think that the layout of the suit is:

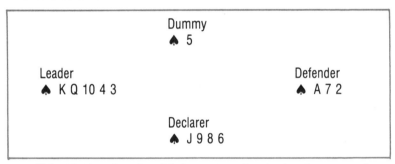

If that is the situation it is important for the leader to continue with a low spade and run five tricks.

But, alas, this is the actual situation, because you *falsecarded*!

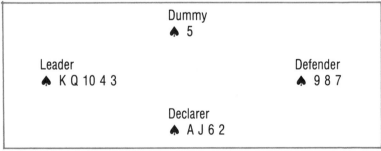

This gives you two tricks in spades instead of one.

You might not have been able to accomplish this ploy if the singleton had been played by dummy and you had to pause for thought at your turn to play.

If you think at your turn to play, and then play low, you reveal that you have the ace and are making a hold-up play. (It is unethical to *pause*, and then play low when you do *not* hold the ace.)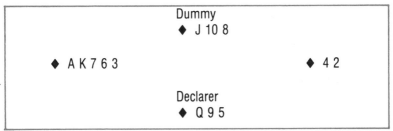

However, when you pause before playing from dummy, the defenders do not know whether you're spending the time planning the hand or thinking about just the first trick.

Anytime you give the opponents an opportunity to take the wrong road, you're well ahead of the game. It's much better than handing them a blueprint to success.

DECLARER DECEPTIVE PLAY

Generally speaking, the term "falsecard" is used only in defensive play. The more correct term for a declarer's attempt to fool the defenders is called "deceptive play." But I'm sure that you and the purists will forgive me if I occasionally use the word "falsecard" when referring to declarer play.

The "Not-So-Obvious" Falsecard

In declarer play, falsecards may succeed if they are subtle enough.

We all use the obvious ones, such as dropping a queen under a king in suit contract play.

	Dummy	
	♦ J 10 8	
♦ A K 7 6 3		♦ 4 2
	Declarer	
	♦ Q 9 5	

Usually, defense signaling can counteract the obvious false-card. When partner plays the ♦ four and declarer plays the ♦ queen, the leader can see that the ♦ two is missing. Either partner has it and is requesting a continuation, or the declarer has it and is falsecarding. In either event it seems safe to continue. In this case, when partner shows up with the deuce on the second round, a third diamond can safely be played for partner to ruff.

So falsecards against good opponents have to be more subtle if they are to be effective.

We all know that in standard defensive attitude signaling you play high-low if you want the suit continued. Well, declarer can do the same thing. When he wants the suit continued he plays high-low! When he wants the suit discontinued he plays low. In either event, he is attempting to give the defensive team a wrong picture of the hand.

EXAMPLE:

```
                    Dummy
                    8 6 4

Leader                          Defender
A K J 3                         10 9 5

                    Declarer
                    Q 7 2
```

In this case, declarer would like the suit continued, so he plays the seven on the king after East plays the five. The leader may think that the unseen hands are:

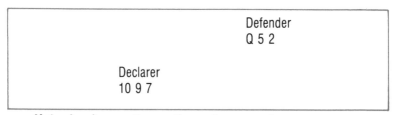

```
                              Defender
                              Q 5 2

            Declarer
            10 9 7
```

If the leader continues the suit you make your queen.

Even if you don't fool the defense this time, they may not continue the suit when the second combination is the actual situation. Always keep 'em guessing!

To Cover or Not to Cover

There are times when you want the opponents to cover your honor lead and there are times you do not want them to do so.

Suppose you, as declarer, have a suit containing a sequence of K Q J. If you want your left-hand opponent to take the first lead of the suit, play the king. If you want him to hold off, play the queen or the jack. Most players capture kings with aces.

Similarly, when you hold Q J 10 etc. in your hand and have ace third in dummy, play the queen when you want your left-hand opponent to cover it and play the jack or ten when you want him to hold off.

TIMING IS EVERYTHING

Being at the right place at the right time is as important in bridge as in other aspects of life.

You want to be in the right hand at the right time. You also want to be in the right contract from the right side. You likewise want to play suits in the right order and cards in the right order, too.

When you do something may be just as essential as *what* you do.

Most of us know that it's often wise to draw trumps and then set up a side suit. There are many occasions, however, where it is vital to set up your side suit *before* you draw trumps.

Here are a few signs to look for to ascertain when this is the case:

1. Do you need the trumps as an entry to the side suit?
2. Do you need to retain trumps in the short hand to prevent loss of trump control in the long hand?
3. Do you need trump entries to take needed finesses in the side suit?

EXAMPLES:
1. *Retaining an entry in dummy.*

```
                North
                ♠ A 8 6
                ♥ 5 4 2
                ♦ K Q J 9
                ♣ 10 9 2
West                              East
♠ 10 3 2                          ♠ 4
♥ Q 6                             ♥ J 10 9 7
♦ 8 5 4                           ♦ A 7 3 2
♣ K Q 7 6 4                       ♣ J 8 5 3
                South
                ♠ K Q J 9 7 5
                ♥ A K 8 3
                ♦ 10 6
                ♣ A
```

Contract: 6♠ by South. Opening lead: ♣king.

South wins the opening lead with his singleton ♣ace, draws two rounds of trump with the king and queen, leaving the ace in dummy. When the suit does not break, declarer *stops* drawing trumps and concentrates on setting up the diamond suit. East holds off to the second round, wins with the ♦ace, and returns another diamond, on which declarer discards a losing heart. Declarer now plays dummy's ace of trump and discards his last heart loser on the set up diamond.

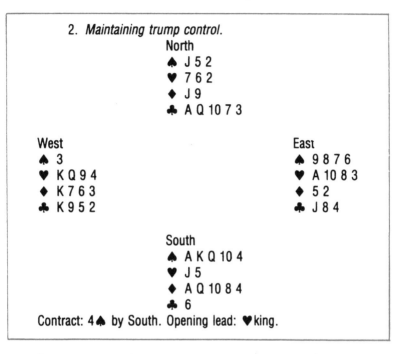

2. *Maintaining trump control.*

North
- ♠ J 5 2
- ♥ 7 6 2
- ♦ J 9
- ♣ A Q 10 7 3

West
- ♠ 3
- ♥ K Q 9 4
- ♦ K 7 6 3
- ♣ K 9 5 2

East
- ♠ 9 8 7 6
- ♥ A 10 8 3
- ♦ 5 2
- ♣ J 8 4

South
- ♠ A K Q 10 4
- ♥ J 5
- ♦ A Q 10 8 4
- ♣ 6

Contract: 4♠ by South. Opening lead: ♥king.

Three rounds of hearts are played, declarer ruffing the third one, reducing South's hand to *four* trumps. Declarer cannot afford to draw trumps.

Now declarer starts on the diamond suit. He leads small to the jack, back to his hand overtaking the nine with the ten and West winning the king (East high-lowed with the five-deuce).

West continues with another diamond, which dummy trumps with the jack. Declarer now draws remaining trumps, and easily scores the balance with his established diamonds.

Notice what would have happened if declarer had drawn two rounds of trump and *then* started on diamonds. True, dummy could ruff the third round with the jack of trumps, but how could declarer get back to his hand?

He would have to play the ♣ace and ruff a club, but this would leave him with only *one* trump and East with *two*. As a result, South would go down two tricks.

3. *Extra trump entries for repeating finesses.*

North
- ♠ K Q 3
- ♥ K 9 7 6
- ♦ 7 5 2
- ♣ 7 6 4

West
- ♠ 8 4
- ♥ Q J 10 3
- ♦ 9 3
- ♣ A K 8 3 2

East
- ♠ 9 5 2
- ♥ A 8 5 2
- ♦ K 10 4
- ♣ J 10 5

South
- ♠ A J 10 7 6
- ♥ 4
- ♦ A Q J 8 6
- ♣ Q 9

Contract: 4♠ by South. Opening lead: ♣king.

South had bid spades and diamonds en route to a four spade contract.

West collected his ♣A K, then switched to the ♥ queen. Declarer now ruffed the second round of hearts.

Declarer thereupon plays the trump ace and a small trump to the queen. A diamond is led from dummy and, when East plays low, South inserts the jack for a successful finesse.

Declarer next draws the opponents' last trump by playing a trump to the king. This enables him to lead a diamond from dummy for the second time. This time he finesses the queen, which wins, and as a result the contract is fulfilled.

WHO SEZ YOU CAN'T COUNT?

For many years the ability to "count a hand" was relegated only to the superexperts. But with a little extra concentration plus our practice sessions, it is an ability that can easily become yours . . . *and what a difference it can make!* It'll make life simpler at the table as well.

Counting the hand can be done equally by both the defenders and the declarer. Counting can usually be done either "inferentially" or "exactly."

By paying attention to the bidding, you can often "infer" the distribution of a particular hand. Suppose you hear an opponent bid a suit, then bid and rebid a different suit. You know that a suit bid and rebid should contain at least five cards. But because another suit was bid first, it should be as long or longer than the second suit bid. Therefore we know that the two suits together contain at least ten cards. That leaves at most only three cards unaccounted for.

So if you hear a player bid "One spade" and then "Two hearts" and "Three hearts," you know he has at least ten cards in spades and hearts, leaving room for a maximum of three cards in clubs and diamonds. If in the course of the play, that player follows to one diamond and ruffs the next one, you know he has at most two clubs.

Once you "know" one unseen hand (plus your own hand and dummy's), you automatically know the distribution of *all* hands. Simple, isn't it? Well, perhaps not *as simple* in execution as in principle . . . but good concentration will bring it off!

When Do I Start Counting?

Counting should start the minute you pick up your hand.

"I have a 4-4-3-2 hand" or "a 4-4-4-1 hand" or "a 6-4-2-1 hand." Counting your own distribution puts you on the right track. It also helps you to make sure you have thirteen cards . . . and thus avoid: "Oops, the ace of spades was hidden."

The next step, of course, is counting your high-card and distributional points to see if, when or how you will participate in the bidding.

From this point on, you start gathering information by listening to the bidding.

You will be receiving mostly two kinds of clues, namely, the distribution of the unseen hands and the high-card strength of those hands. These bits of information will help guide you in bidding decisions as well as in your subsequent play.

Let's see how it all works.

With North the dealer, the bidding went along reasonably normal lines:

North			
♠ Q J 9 3			
♥ 8 5 4			
♦ A Q 6			
♣ A 10 3			

South
♠ A K 10 7 4
♥ Q 7
♦ J 10 2
♣ K J 9

THE BIDDING:

North	East	South	West
1 ♣	1 ♥	1 ♠	Pass
2 ♠	3 ♥	4 ♠	Pass
Pass	Pass		

OPENING LEAD: ♥ nine

Now place yourself in declarer's seat. From the sound of the bidding, East appears to have at least a six-card heart suit. That's all the information you have at the moment.

East wins the first trick with the heart king and continues the ace, on which West plays the three. East now continues with the jack. It seems obvious that West originally had only two hearts, so you ruff with the ten, West discarding a low club. You have now completely confirmed that East originally held six hearts. Keep that on the backburner of your brain.

You now start to draw trumps. Small spade to the queen, both defenders follow. On the second lead of trumps to your king, East follows suit but West discards another club. Aha! East originally held three spades. You now know nine of East's cards. You next draw his last trump with your ace, West discarding still another club.

You maneuvered to keep the lead in your hand so you could try a diamond finesse. Your diamond jack loses to East's king and he returns a diamond to dummy's queen. The ace of diamonds is now played and everybody follows suit.

Your only concern now is to avoid a loser in clubs, where there is a two-way finesse. Which way do you go?

Well, if you've been counting there is no problem. East just followed to all three diamond plays. Add that to his nine cards in hearts and spades and you know *twelve* of his cards. At most, he has one club.

You therefore lead a club to your king. If East has the queen, it will fall under your king. If not, you take a sure finesse against West's queen of clubs.

The count of the hand has made a sure thing out of a fifty-fifty guess.

Here is the complete hand:

```
                    North
                    ♠ Q J 9 3
                    ♥ 8 5 4
                    ♦ A Q 6
                    ♣ A 10 3

West                                      East
♠ 8                                       ♠ 6 5 2
♥ 9 3                                     ♥ A K J 10 6 2
♦ 9 8 5 3                                 ♦ K 7 4
♣ Q 8 7 6 5 4                             ♣ 2

                    South
                    ♠ A K 10 7 4
                    ♥ Q 7
                    ♦ J 10 2
                    ♣ K J 9
```

CHANGING HORSES IN MIDSTREAM

The best laid plans of mice and bridge players ofttimes go astray. The ability to maneuver under these circumstances is an art unto itself.

Of course, having alternate plans in anticipation of problems is the best method of circumventing unexpected developments.

Let us examine this situation:

```
                    North
                    ♠ A J 10 7
                    ♥ 7 6
                    ♦ Q J 7 6 2
                    ♣ 8 6

                    South
                    ♠ K Q 9 8
                    ♥ A 8 5
                    ♦ K 8
                    ♣ A 9 7 5
```

BIDDING:

South	West	North	East
1 NT	Pass	2 ♣	Pass
2 ♠	Pass	4 ♠	Pass
Pass	Pass		

OPENING LEAD: ♣king.

After a one notrump opening bid, a Stayman auction placed South in a four spade contract.

Planning the hand upon viewing the opening lead, declarer realizes he has two ways to go. He can either set up the diamond suit or play the hand as a crossruff.

He figures that the ruffing route is the safest plan. It doesn't require a normal three-two break in trumps. Three ruffs in the South hand, three high-card winners in clubs, diamonds and hearts plus four top trump tricks in the North hand add up to a ten-trick total.

To help retain control of the hand and keep his options open, South holds off winning the first trick.

West, sensing declarer's plan, switches to a trump. The trick is won in dummy with the ten, and a small diamond is led to South's king.

West wins with the ace and returns another trump, throwing declarer's ruffing plan into the trash can.

Declarer now has to *switch tactics*. He has to try to set up the diamond suit. As East follows suit, declarer wins the trump return in his hand. He plays his remaining diamond to dummy's queen, both opponents following.

As the diamond suit is sure to break no worse than four-two, it is now safe to draw the outstanding trump. The ♠ ace is played from the North hand, followed by the ♦ jack.

If the diamonds break three-three, eleven tricks are now certain. If they divide four-two, a small diamond is then ruffed in the South hand. This sets up North's fifth diamond as a winner. Declarer winds up making four spades, losing a heart, diamond and a club.

This is the complete hand:

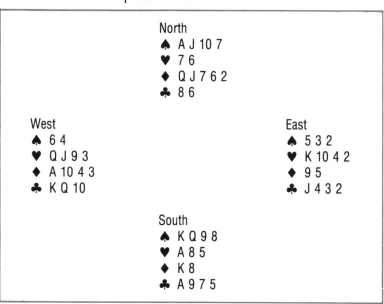

North
♠ A J 10 7
♥ 7 6
♦ Q J 7 6 2
♣ 8 6

West
♠ 6 4
♥ Q J 9 3
♦ A 10 4 3
♣ K Q 10

East
♠ 5 3 2
♥ K 10 4 2
♦ 9 5
♣ J 4 3 2

South
♠ K Q 9 8
♥ A 8 5
♦ K 8
♣ A 9 7 5

Declarer truly swapped horses in midstream. But after selecting the ruffing route first, he was able to switch to another tactic when the initial option was thwarted.

SAFETY PLAYS

In the old days, a cautious person was described as one who wore a belt *and* suspenders.

In declarer play, there are many precautions that can be taken. Some cost nothing at all. Others may cost a trick, but if it insures the contract it is often well worth it (unless you're playing match-point duplicate).

Safety plays are too numerous to cover here completely. So we'll serve up a few hors d'oeuvres just to give us a taste of them. Hopefully it will heighten our awareness and help us to recognize safety-play opportunities when they occur.

Here are two "look-alikes":

HAND A.	DUMMY A 10 6 3	HAND B.	DUMMY A 8 6 3
	YOU K Q 9 7 2		YOU K Q 9 7 2

In each of these examples the problem is to avoid losing a trick if one of the opponents holds all four of the outstanding cards.

HAND A: You have a 100 percent certainty of winning five tricks in the suit. Play the king first. If one opponent shows out, you can safely finesse against the other opponent's jack. You still have the ace-ten in dummy and the queen-nine in your hand.

HAND B: Do *not* play the king first. Play the deuce to dummy's ace. If your left-hand opponent shows out, you are able to finesse against the other opponent's remaining J 10 5, with your K Q 9 7. (Lead small from dummy, cover the ten with your queen. Reenter dummy in another suit and finesse again against the jack.)

Against a four-zero break in this hand you had only a 50 percent chance. If your left-hand opponent held all four cards you could do nothing about it.

If your right-hand opponent held all four cards, you could trap them all with correct play.

The key item to recognize in Hand B is that you are missing *both the jack and the ten*. It is therefore necessary to retain *two honors* over them.

HAND C. DUMMY	HAND D. DUMMY
A K Q 6 4	A K Q 6 4 3
YOU	YOU
7 5	7 5

Here are two cases where there are no outside entries to dummy. In each case you can afford to give up one trick and still make your contract.

HAND C: In either duplicate or rubber bridge, the proper play is to give up a trick to the opponents immediately. This guards against a four-two break. The odds are that the four-two break will occur about 48 percent of the time. A three-three division will happen about 36 percent of the time.

HAND D: With only five cards outstanding, it is still wise to give up a trick immediately and guard against a four-one break. The safety of the contract is paramount.

(The only exception is in match-point duplicate where over-tricks are so important. The odds favoring a three-two break, about 68 percent, are good enough to justify the risk.)

When it comes to safety plays, to finesse or not to finesse is often the question.

In each of the following situations you can afford to lose one trick but not two. How do you handle them?

HAND E.	NORTH (DUMMY) A 9 3 2	HAND F.	NORTH (DUMMY) 7 6 3
	SOUTH (YOU) K 10 7 6 3		SOUTH (YOU) A Q 10 9 5 4

HAND E: The only way you can lose two tricks is if one opponent holds all four outstanding cards, Q J 8 4. To guard against this possibility, a safety play can be employed. Lead a small card toward dummy. If a small card is played by West, finesse the nine. If it loses to East, you know the suit will break no worse than three-one and your ace-king will pick up the outstanding cards. If the nine holds and East shows out, you eventually lose only one trick to West.

If West shows out on the first play of the suit, you can still play the nine, losing to East's jack. Win any return, play North's ace and take the proven finesse against East's queen.

HAND F: This is a card combination where it is easy to go astray.

If West holds three or four cards headed by the king-jack, there is no way to avoid losing two tricks. When this is not the case, however, a safety play may take the guess out of the hand.

Lead the seven from dummy. If a small card is played by East, *do not finesse*, play the ace. If an honor is played by West, you are home free. If it is the jack, you simply surrender a trick to the king. If it is the king that fell under your ace, you've gained a "bonus trick," because you can reenter dummy in another suit, and finesse East for the missing jack.

If, when you played the ace, West followed low or showed out, return to dummy in another suit, and lead the six. You now cover whatever East plays. (If West originally showed out, you have to reach dummy one more time and lead up to your hand again.) In any event, you lose only to the opponent's king.

Of course, if on your first lead East played an honor, simply cover it. If the jack was played cover with the queen; if it was the king, play the ace. The most you can now lose is one trick.

In Hand E, the safety play was to take a first-round finesse. In Hand F, the safety play was to refuse to take the first-round finesse.

THE STRIP AND END PLAY

The definition of a pseudoexpert is a person whose mission in life is to make a grand slam contract by means of a strip and end play.

As the technique of the play includes *losing a trick* to a defender at a time when he cannot make a safe exit, we have serious doubts that our "expert friend" will ever achieve his goal. But the ability to execute a strip and end play is well within the reach of the average player. Since the opportunity to make the play comes up quite often, it should be in the arsenal of every good player.

The most important factor is to be able to recognize the conditions when the use of a strip and end play is feasible.

Here are some of the more prevalent types of strip-and-end-play hands.

HAND 1. *Avoiding a guess in a two-way finesse situation.*

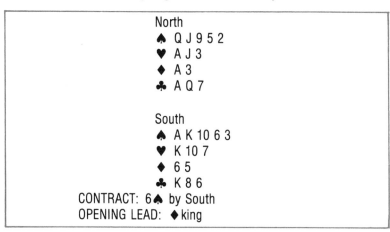

North
♠ Q J 9 5 2
♥ A J 3
♦ A 3
♣ A Q 7

South
♠ A K 10 6 3
♥ K 10 7
♦ 6 5
♣ K 8 6
CONTRACT: 6♠ by South
OPENING LEAD: ♦ king

In this hand you have eleven tricks available, off the top. For your twelfth trick, you either can try to guess the location of the ♥ queen, a 50 percent chance, or you can execute a strip and end play, a 100 percent sure thing. The technique on this hand is: Win the opening lead, draw the outstanding trumps and play all your clubs, which leaves this setup:

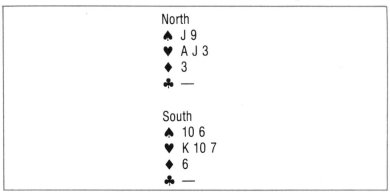

North
♠ J 9
♥ A J 3
♦ 3
♣ —

South
♠ 10 6
♥ K 10 7
♦ 6
♣ —

You now play your last diamond, which completes the stripping part of the play and places an opponent on lead. He must now return a heart, which gives you a free finesse, or a diamond or club which you ruff in one hand as you sluff a heart in the other. In either event, you get your twelfth trick.

See the complete hand on the next page. Switch the ♥ queen from East to West, if you like. The end play always works.

North
♠ Q J 9 5 2
♥ A J 3
♦ A 3
♣ A Q 7

West
♠ 8 4
♥ 9 6 4
♦ K Q J 9 4
♣ J 9 4

East
♠ 7
♥ Q 8 5 2
♦ 10 8 7 2
♣ 10 5 3 2

South
♠ A K 10 6 3
♥ K 10 7
♦ 6 5
♣ K 8 6

HAND 2. *Avoiding a guess by "ducking."*

North
♠ A K 4
♥ Q 10 7 4
♦ 8 7 3
♣ 7 6 3

South
♠ Q 7 6
♥ A K J 6 3
♦ 6 2
♣ A Q 9

CONTRACT: 4♥ by South
OPENING LEAD: ♦ king

The opponents play the king, ace, queen of diamonds, which you ruff. Draw the trumps (let's assume they break three-one, or two-two), then play three rounds of spades winding up in dummy and *stripping* the hand.

This is now the situation:

North
♠ —
♥ 10
♦ —
♣ 7 6 3

South
♠ —
♥ J
♦ —
♣ A Q 9

A small club is led from dummy. If East plays small,* play the nine. This *ends* up placing West in the lead, who must either play a club into your ace-queen, or lead a spade or a diamond giving you a ruff and a sluff.

Here's the entire hand:

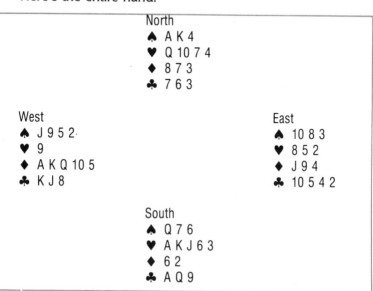

North
♠ A K 4
♥ Q 10 7 4
♦ 8 7 3
♣ 7 6 3

West
♠ J 9 5 2
♥ 9
♦ A K Q 10 5
♣ K J 8

East
♠ 10 8 3
♥ 8 5 2
♦ J 9 4
♣ 10 5 4 2

South
♠ Q 7 6
♥ A K J 6 3
♦ 6 2
♣ A Q 9

* If East plays either the jack or ten, you cover with your queen, making your ace-nine a tenace position.

(A little defensive note: Whenever you are in the same situation as East, it is wise to insert a high card such as a jack or ten, instead of playing second-hand low. If declarer does not hold the nine, you can thwart the end play.)

HAND 3. *Putting the safe opponent into the lead via a "known" card.*

North
♠ Q J 9 4 3
♥ A 7
♦ 9 6 3
♣ K Q 6

South
♠ A K 10 5 2
♥ J 5
♦ A Q
♣ A 7 4 2

CONTRACT: 6♠ by South
OPENING LEAD: ♥king

Win the opening lead with the ♥ace and draw trumps. Play the king, queen and ace of clubs. If the suit does not break evenly, ruff your last club in dummy.

This is now the situation:

```
                    North
                    ♠ Q
                    ♥ 7
                    ♦ 9 6 3
                    ♣ —

                    South
                    ♠ 5 2
                    ♥ J
                    ♦ A Q
                    ♣ —
```

The play of the ♥ seven to the ♥ jack strips the hand and places West into the lead with his "known" ♥ queen. He must either return a diamond into your ace-queen, or a heart or a club which you trump in dummy, enabling you to discard your ♦ queen.

This is the entire hand:

```
                    North
                    ♠ Q J 9 4 3
                    ♥ A 7
                    ♦ 9 6 3
                    ♣ K Q 6

West                                    East
♠ —                                     ♠ 8 7 6
♥ K Q 10 9 6                            ♥ 8 4 3 2
♦ K 10 7 4                              ♦ J 8 5 2
♣ J 10 8 3                              ♣ 9 5

                    South
                    ♠ A K 10 5 2
                    ♥ J 5
                    ♦ A Q
                    ♣ A 7 4 2
```

HAND 4. *Discarding a loser on a card which will put the safe opponent on lead.*

North
♠ 6 3 2
♥ A J 3
♦ K J 10 8 5
♣ 7 4

South
♠ A Q 4
♥ 2
♦ A Q 9 6 4
♣ A K 6 5

CONTRACT: 6♦ by South
OPENING LEAD: ♥ king

Win the opening lead with the ♥ ace. Play two rounds of trumps, hoping this will draw the opponents' trumps. Play the ace, king and a third club which you ruff in dummy. Then ruff a small heart in your hand and your last club in dummy.

This is now the situation:

North
♠ 6 3 2
♥ J
♦ 10
♣ —

South
♠ A Q 4
♥ —
♦ 9 6
♣ —

Lead the ♥jack, discarding your ♠four. This strips the hand and places West into the lead with his "known" ♥queen. West now has the unenviable choice of playing a spade into your ace-queen or playing one of your void suits which you will ruff in dummy while discarding the ♠queen from your hand.

Here's the complete hand:

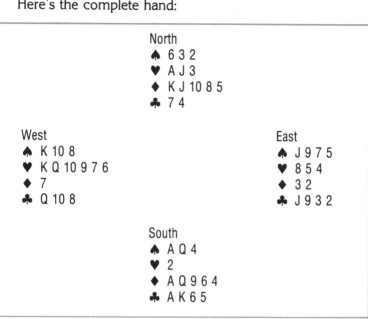

North
♠ 6 3 2
♥ A J 3
♦ K J 10 8 5
♣ 7 4

West
♠ K 10 8
♥ K Q 10 9 7 6
♦ 7
♣ Q 10 8

East
♠ J 9 7 5
♥ 8 5 4
♦ 3 2
♣ J 9 3 2

South
♠ A Q 4
♥ 2
♦ A Q 9 6 4
♣ A K 6 5

HAND 5. *Getting a 50 percent chance of making an otherwise unmakable contract.*

North
♠ Q 3
♥ A J
♦ K J 7 5
♣ Q 10 6 3 2

South
♣ A 6
♥ 8 6
♦ A Q 6 4
♣ A K J 7 4

CONTRACT: 6♣ by South
OPENING LEAD: ♥ king
(West bid hearts along the way.)

Up until now we've been illustrating hands in which the strip and end play virtually guarantees the contract. In view of the bidding, the strip and end play in this hand has a good chance of bringing home the slam, but there are no guarantees.

Win the opening lead with your ♥ ace. Draw the opponents' trumps and cash all your diamonds.

This is now the situation:

North
♠ Q 3
♥ J
♦ —
♣ 10 6

South
♠ A 6
♥ 8
♦ —
♣ J 7

Play the ♥ jack which completes the stripping aspect and places West into the lead with the ♥ queen. West must play a spade, otherwise you get a ruff and a sluff, guaranteeing your contract. When he *does* lead a small spade, play the queen. If West holds the ♠king, you make your contract. If not, down you go.

This is the complete hand:

North
♠ Q 3
♥ A J
♦ K J 7 5
♣ Q 10 6 3 2

West
♠ K 9 7 2
♥ K Q 10 9 7 5
♦ 10 8 2
♣ —

East
♠ J 10 8 5 4
♥ 4 3 2
♦ 9 3
♣ 9 8 5

South
♠ A 6
♥ 8 6
♦ A Q 6 4
♣ A K J 7 4

NO RUFF 'N' SLUFF...
BUT I GOTCHA
IN THE END,
ANYWAY!

This tactic is possible in notrump as well as in suit contracts. The main difference is that you do not have a trump suit as a stopper, and hence no ruff and sluff possibilities.

HAND 6. *The strip and end play in notrump contracts.*

```
                        North
                        ♠ 7 4 3
                        ♥ 8 7 6
                        ♦ A J 6
                        ♣ K Q J 4

                        South
                        ♠ A 6 5 2
                        ♥ A Q
                        ♦ K 10 7
                        ♣ A 7 6 5
        CONTRACT: 3 NT by South
        OPENING LEAD: ♠king
```

As West leads the ♠king, you count that you have eight winners off the top. You hold up, winning the third spade round as East shows out. Cash your four club tricks making sure to wind up in your hand. This strips West of the club suit.

This is now the situation:

```
                        North
                        ♠ —
                        ♥ 8 7 6
                        ♦ A J 6
                        ♣ —

                        South
                        ♠ 8
                        ♥ A Q
                        ♦ K 10 7
                        ♣ —
```

Play the ♠eight from your hand, discarding a small heart from dummy, which puts West into the lead. He now must play a diamond or a heart (that's all he's got) and your contract is assured. As a matter of fact, you also have a safe chance for an overtrick by taking a finesse in the suit that was not led.

Here's the entire hand:

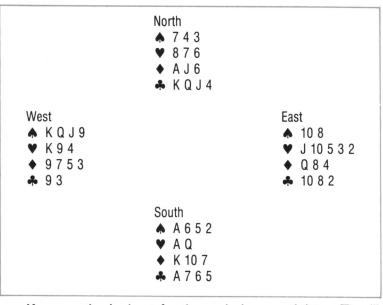

North
♠ 7 4 3
♥ 8 7 6
♦ A J 6
♣ K Q J 4

West
♠ K Q J 9
♥ K 9 4
♦ 9 7 5 3
♣ 9 3

East
♠ 10 8
♥ J 10 5 3 2
♦ Q 8 4
♣ 10 8 2

South
♠ A 6 5 2
♥ A Q
♦ K 10 7
♣ A 7 6 5

Keep on the lookout for the end-play possibilities. They'll save you tricks and help you fulfill many otherwise unmakable contracts.

WHO, ME? THREATEN YOU?...

...JUST FOR ONE MEASLY TRICK?

OUCH! THIS SQUEEZE DOESN'T FEEL SIMPLE!

H·L.

THE SQUEEZE PLAY

Another tool that should be in the hands of every successful bridge player is the squeeze play. There are many varieties of the squeeze play and several fat books have been written solely on this subject.

But the ability to execute a simple squeeze is well within the scope of most competent bridge players. So let's cover the minimum requirements of the play.

1. You should be able to win all the remaining tricks except one.
2. One opponent must guard at least two suits.
3. Your side holds "menace" or "threat" cards in these two suits.
4. You hold a winner in a third suit—"the squeeze card"—which forces the opponent to make a losing discard.
5. When the squeeze card is led, the opponent does not have an idle card to discard. He must discard in one of the vital suits.

Here are a couple of end positions, to give you an idea how the simple squeeze works:

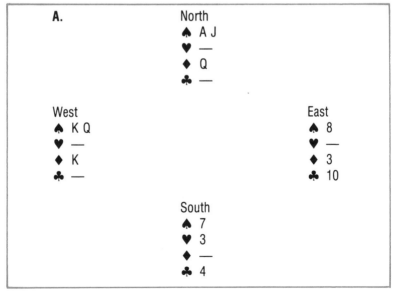

```
              A.           North
                           ♠ A J
                           ♥ —
                           ♦ Q
                           ♣ —

West                                        East
♠ K Q                                       ♠ 8
♥ —                                         ♥ —
♦ K                                         ♦ 3
♣ —                                         ♣ 10

                           South
                           ♠ 7
                           ♥ 3
                           ♦ —
                           ♣ 4
```

South leads the ♥ three—"the squeeze card." West cannot discard the ♦ king, it would set up North's queen. If West discards the ♠queen, North discards the ♦queen, and then leads a spade to North's ace-jack.

You will note that in this example, North held *both* "threat cards," the ♦queen and the ♠jack. It was therefore necessary for North to discard *after* the squeezed opponent, West, discarded.

B.

```
                    North
                    ♠ —
                    ♥ A J
                    ♦ 3
                    ♣ —

West                                    East
♠ —                                     ♠ —
♥ 10                                    ♥ K Q
♦ 7 6                                   ♦ K
♣ —                                     ♣ —

                    South
                    ♠ A
                    ♥ 3
                    ♦ Q
                    ♣ —
```

In this example, where the threat cards are not in the same hand, it is possible to discard from dummy *before* the opponent gets squeezed.

South leads the ♠ace. West's discard is immaterial. North discards the ♦three and East is squeezed. If the ♦king is discarded, South cashes the ♦queen, discarding the ♥jack in North. If the ♥queen is discarded, South leads a heart to North's ace-jack.

You will note in both examples, it was necessary for South to have at least *one* card to reach the two-card menace combination in the North hand. When the squeeze card is led, declarer must have communication from one hand to the other.

To obtain a better view of the squeeze potentials, let's examine some complete hands.

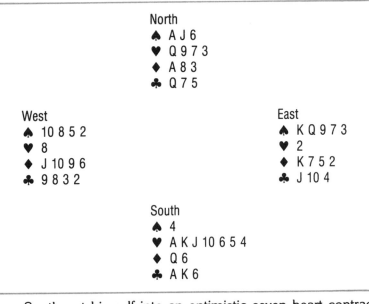

North
♠ A J 6
♥ Q 9 7 3
♦ A 8 3
♣ Q 7 5

West
♠ 10 8 5 2
♥ 8
♦ J 10 9 6
♣ 9 8 3 2

East
♠ K Q 9 7 3
♥ 2
♦ K 7 5 2
♣ J 10 4

South
♠ 4
♥ A K J 10 6 5 4
♦ Q 6
♣ A K 6

South got himself into an optimistic seven heart contract and West led the ♦jack. South could count twelve tricks off the top and felt that West would not have led from a king-jack combination against a grand slam contract. The only chance was a squeeze against East in the spade and diamond suits. He, therefore, rose with the ♦ace, drew trumps and cashed his three club tricks. He then played all his trumps except one, arriving at this position:

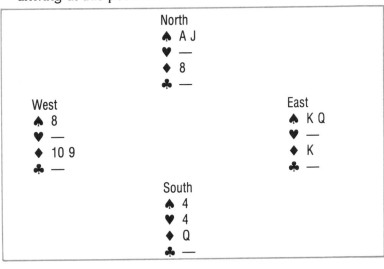

North
♠ A J
♥ —
♦ 8
♣ —

West
♠ 8
♥ —
♦ 10 9
♣ —

East
♠ K Q
♥ —
♦ K
♣ —

South
♠ 4
♥ 4
♦ Q
♣ —

South now led the last trump. West's discard was immaterial and the ♦ eight was discarded from the North hand. East had the unenviable choice of discarding the ♦ king, thereby setting up South's ♦ queen or discarding the ♠ queen permitting declarer to drop the king under his ♠ ace.

However, if you were to switch the East and West hands, and a normal opening lead of the ♠ king is made, you wind up with a squeeze against West. This would be the end position:

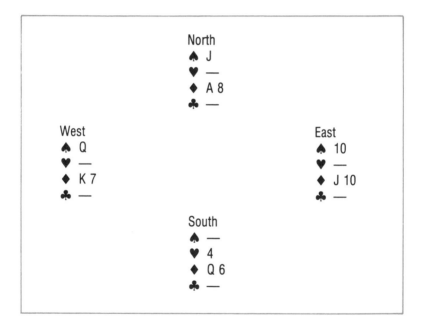

```
                    North
                    ♠  J
                    ♥  —
                    ♦  A 8
                    ♣  —
West                                    East
♠  Q                                    ♠  10
♥  —                                    ♥  —
♦  K 7                                  ♦  J 10
♣  —                                    ♣  —
                    South
                    ♠  —
                    ♥  4
                    ♦  Q 6
                    ♣  —
```

The lead of the ♥ four squeezes West. If he discards the ♠ queen, it sets up the ♠ jack and North, therefore, discards the ♦ eight. If West discards the ♦ seven, the ♠ jack is discarded from the North hand. This permits the ♦ ace to gobble up West's ♦ king; making South's ♦ queen a winner.

Squeeze plays are effective not only for slam contracts, but also for modest game and even part-score efforts.

Example:

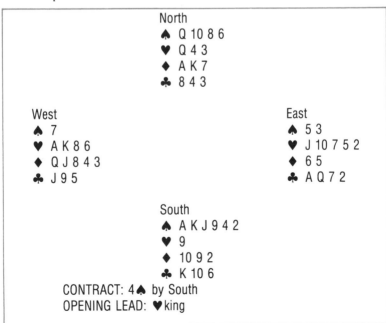

North
♠ Q 10 8 6
♥ Q 4 3
♦ A K 7
♣ 8 4 3

West
♠ 7
♥ A K 8 6
♦ Q J 8 4 3
♣ J 9 5

East
♠ 5 3
♥ J 10 7 5 2
♦ 6 5
♣ A Q 7 2

South
♠ A K J 9 4 2
♥ 9
♦ 10 9 2
♣ K 10 6

CONTRACT: 4♠ by South
OPENING LEAD: ♥king

After West leads the ♥ king, East playing the deuce, he switches to a club. East wins the ace and returns a club, South winning the king. South draws the outstanding trumps and exits with a club, East winning with the queen. The defenders now have their book. East plays a heart and South ruffs.

Note that at this point declarer has all the remaining tricks except one. He therefore tries to execute a squeeze for the game-going trick. Accordingly, he plays all his trumps but one and comes to this position:

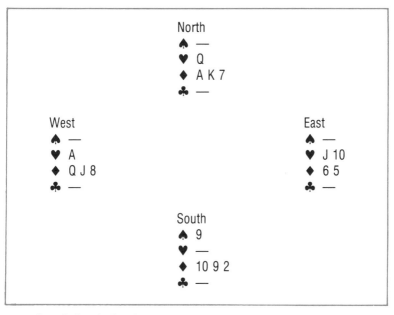

North
♠ —
♥ Q
♦ A K 7
♣ —

West
♠ —
♥ A
♦ Q J 8
♣ —

East
♠ —
♥ J 10
♦ 6 5
♣ —

South
♠ 9
♥ —
♦ 10 9 2
♣ —

South leads his last trump which squeezes West. A ♥ ace discard sets up dummy's queen. A diamond discard permits declarer to discard the ♥ queen, thereby setting up the third diamond for the last trick.

A bit of advice: Whenever you are within a trick of your contract and you have a long suit to run . . . *run it down, whenever you can safely do so.* Even if you don't have a true squeeze, defenders are human and they may err. They often *do* discard improperly or they *believe* they are being squeezed. This is called a pseudosqueeze. You can often pick up unexpected tricks this way.

RESTRICTED CHOICE

The principle of Restricted Choice comes up in play situations such as this:

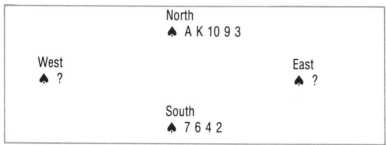

North
♠ A K 10 9 3

West
♠ ?

East
♠ ?

South
♠ 7 6 4 2

You, South, lead the deuce, West plays the five, North plays the king and East plays the "Quack." That is: either the queen or the jack.

If East held *both* cards, he had a choice of playing either the queen or the jack. But on the other hand, East may have played the "quack" because he had no other choice. He had to play it. It was the only card in the suit he held.

The recommended play, therefore, is for South to return to his hand in another suit and lead a small spade. When West plays the ♠ eight, North finesses with the nine spot. East is more likely to have held a singleton honor than specifically both the queen and jack. The odds are almost 2-to-1 that the finesse will succeed.

The Official Encyclopedia of Bridge defines Restricted Choice as follows:

> "The play of a card which may have been selected as a choice of equal plays increases the chance that the player started with a holding in which his choice was restricted."

Another example of the application of the Restricted Choice principle is this situation:

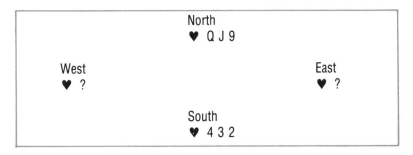

North
♥ Q J 9

West
♥ ?

East
♥ ?

South
♥ 4 3 2

South leads a small heart, small from West, jack from dummy and East wins with the king. Upon obtaining the lead again South now leads with another small heart, small from West . . . *Which card should be played from dummy, the queen or the nine?*

The principle of Restricted Choice says that West is more likely to hold the ace, rather than East. Therefore the queen should be played.

Why? Originally East could have won the first trick with *either* the ace or the king, if he held both these cards. But the greater likelihood is, he won with the king because he *had* to. His choice was restricted. Again, the odds are almost 2-to-1 in your favor.

Like everything else, the use of this principle has to be applied with judgment. Point count and distributional analysis of the opponents' hands as a result of bidding and previous play may alter your actions.

An excellent analysis of Restricted Choice is extensively covered in *The Official Encyclopedia of Bridge.*

BIDDING

THE MAGIC OF THE LIMIT BID

There are very few bidding concepts that hold true no matter what style or what system you use. But here is one that is sure to work. Understanding whether one has made a limit or un-limited bid opens many doors for you and makes life much simpler at the bridge table.

Let's define the terms.

LIMIT BID: A bid that describes the strength of a hand within a *narrow limited range.*

A LIMIT BID
DESCRIBES THE STRENGTH OF A HAND WITHIN A
NARROW LIMITED RANGE
EXAMPLES:
6 to 9 PTS.
13 to 15 PTS.
16 to 18 PTS.
H.L.

The opening one notrump bid is, in virtually all systems, a prime example of a limit bid.

In Standard American it is: 16 to 18 points. Or, if you are one of those who modify it, it is perhaps: 15 to 17 points.

The weak notrumpers have it as: 11 to 13 points, 12 to 14 points, or 13 to 15 points.

Whatever your system, it is still a limit bid. You know within a narrow range of 2 to 3 points the strength of the opening one notrump bid.

Two notrump opening bids are similarly limit bids. Although they are strong bids (22 to 24 points, 21 to 23 points, or 20 to 22 points, depending upon your style) they are still limit bids.

Likewise, certain *responses* are limit bids.

In Standard American, for example, a response of two spades to partner's one spade opening bid is a limit bid. It indicates 6 to 9 points (occasionally 10). Or a response of one notrump to an opening suit bid also shows 6 to 9 points (occasionally 10).

A three heart response to partner's one heart opening bid,

although it is forcing, is a limit bid of 13 to 15 points, including distributional values.

(If you are one who plays nonforcing limit jump raises, a three spade response to an opening one spade bid indicates 10 to 12 points or 9 to 11 points depending upon your style. Again, a limit bid.)

If you passed originally, any response you make to partner's opening bid is a limit bid. The fact that you did not open limits your hand to 12 or less points.

So what is an UNLIMITED BID?

The UNLIMITED BID
WE MAY KNOW THE BOTTOM... ...BUT WE DON'T KNOW THE TOP!

An unlimited bid is one that indicates the bottom strength of the hand but not the top.

In standard practice, an opening bid of one in a suit is an unlimited bid. It could be as low as 12 to 13 points or as high as 20 or more points.

A response of one spade (by an unpassed hand) over partner's opening bid of one club, diamond or heart, is an unlimited bid. It could be as low as 6 points or as high as 20!

A response of two clubs, over partner's opening one diamond, heart or spade bid, is likewise an unlimited bid . . . as low as 10 points or as high as 20!

In all these examples we have a fairly good idea of the bottom limits of the hand, but not the top, hence they are all *unlimited bids.*

Who's the Captain?

Your partner has just made a limit bid. Who becomes the captain of your partnership?

You know within a couple of points the strength of your partner's hand. You are, therefore, in the best position to make decisions. That makes you the captain.

By definition, then, the partner of the limit bidder becomes the captain.

Strength really has no bearing on who's captain. Sometimes it is the strong hand; sometimes it is the weak hand.

You open with a 2 NT bid. You are the *strong* hand . . . but your *partner* is the captain.

You open with 1 ♥. Partner responds 2 ♥. This time, again, you have the strong hand. But this time *you're* the captain. Partner has made the limit bid.

1.   East is the captain. Partner's 1 NT bid is limited. East, as captain, decided that the hand should be played in a 2 ♥ part score. West should now pass.

2. West is the captain. East's 2♠ bid is limited. Depending upon his hand, West can pass with a minimum hand, jump to 4♠ with a 19 point-plus hand, or probe for game with an in-between hand.

3. West is the captain. East's 3♥ bid, although game-forcing in standard bidding, is limited to 13 to 15 points. West simply bids 4♥ with a minimum hand or probes for slam with a good hand containing slam potential.

4. East is the captain. West by his original pass has made his 2♣ call a limit bid. East can take whatever action is appropriate for her hand, including a pass.

WHEN YOU ARE CAPTAIN, SOMETIMES YOU ARE **SURE** WHERE YOU WANT TO BE... **SO YOU JUST UP AND BID IT!**

Now that you're the captain, where do you go from here? Sometimes you are "sure" where you want to be . . . *so you just up and bid it!*

1. Over partner's 1 NT bid, if you know where you want to wind up, just bid it.

  With a poor balanced hand, pass. With a poor unbalanced hand, bid 2♦, 2♥ or 2♠ as the hand requires. (Of course, if you're playing Jacoby transfers, use the appropriate bid for landing in a 2♥ or 2♠ contract.)

  With good balanced hands: Bid 3 NT with a 10 point-plus hand; bid 6 NT with a 17 or 18 point hand.

  With a good hand containing a six card major suit you can bid 4♥ or 4♠ (or the appropriate Texas transfer bid). Or even slam can be bid with the appropriate strength and controls.

2. Over partner's 2♠ response, pass with a minimum, bid 4♠ with a 19 point-plus hand.

You are not always certain where you want to be. Here you pass the buck back to your partner.

Over partner's 1 NT opening bid, for example, with an eight to nine point balanced hand you bid 2 NT, asking partner to bid 3 NT with a maximum or to pass with a minimum.

Or over partner's 1 NT opener, you may have a very good balanced hand of 15 to 16 points. You bid 4 NT asking partner to bid 6 NT with a maximum or to pass with a minimum.

Sometimes, over partner's opening 1 NT, you're not sure whether to play the hand in notrump or in a major suit. That's where the Stayman convention comes in.

Over a 1 ♥, 2 ♥ sequence, you can make a game try by bidding another suit. Partner can return to 3 ♥ with a minimum hand or jump to 4 ♥ with a good fitting hand.

Answers Many Questions

Understanding the difference between limit and unlimited bids answers many questions.

"How come, when partner opens with one of a suit, I have to *bid* with as little as 6 points, yet when he opens with a *strong* one notrump bid, I may *pass* with as much as 7 points?"

In Standard American an opening bid of one in a suit can be as low as 13 points, but it can also be as high as 20 points. It is an unlimited bid. You have to respond with 6 points to allow for these possibilities.

The one notrump bid, though strong, is limited to an 18 point maximum. Therefore you may pass with 7 points.

"Why is a new suit bid by a responder, who has never previously passed, forcing?"

It is true that partner's response in a new suit at the one level can be based on a hand with as little as 6 points. But it also can be based on a hand containing even as much as 20 points. It is unlimited and therefore forcing.

So, from now on, whenever partner makes a bid, first ask yourself: Is it a limit bid or an unlimited bid? You'll be surprised how things begin to fall into place.

FOR BETTER OR FOR WORSE

In evaluating their hands, most players rely heavily on their point count.

What we'd like to stress here is that hand evaluation is not a static thing. As the bidding proceeds, things get better or things get worse.

When you are at the table, no one else can do this evaluation except you. What I'd like to do is merely create an awareness of this concept, so that you will be better equipped to make correct decisions at the table.

Let's take a look at this truly average hand. You hold 10 high-card points:

♠ A 8 6 2
♥ K 9 5
♦ Q J
♣ 10 7 4 3

If the opponents bid diamonds, your queen-jack may be no better than a trey-deuce. They may be gobbled up by the opponents' ace-king.

If your partner bids diamonds and has the ace-king, the queen-jack become equivalent to his ace-king. They supply two tricks for your side.

If your right-hand opponent bids hearts, your king becomes golden. It is sitting behind the opponent's presumed ace. However, if your left-hand adversary bids hearts, your king could go bye-bye.

How do these changes in evaluation influence bidding?

Holding that very same hand, let's see what your rebids would be in these two auctions:

A.	PTNR	OPP'T	YOU	OPP'T
	1 ♥	Pass	1 ♠	Pass
	2 ♦	Pass	?	

B.	PTNR	OPP'T	YOU	OPP'T
	1 ♥	Pass	1 ♠	Pass
	2 ♣	Pass	?	

In sequence A, your queen and jack of diamonds are working for you. A jump preference to 3 ♥ describes your improved hand. Partner is invited to continue to game.

In sequence B, the value of your diamond holding is unclear. A simple preference to 2 ♥ is indicated.

Here are two hands partner might have for his bids:

A. PARTNER	B. PARTNER
♠ 7 5	♠ 7 5
♥ A Q 10 6 4	♥ A Q 10 6 4
♦ A K 6 2	♦ 6 5
♣ 6 5	♣ A K 6 2
YOU	YOU
♠ A 8 6 2	♠ A 8 6 2
♥ K 9 5	♥ K 9 5
♦ Q J	♦ Q J
♣ 10 7 4 3	♣ 10 7 4 3

In Hand A, your diamond holding solidifies his side suit and makes a game contract in hearts a very good venture.

In Hand B, with the clubs and diamonds interchanged, four hearts is a virtually hopeless contract.

In the following hand you are South and your partner opens the bidding with 1♠. You hold:

♠ Q 8
♥ Q 10 6 5 3
♦ A 6 5
♣ 8 7 5

Playing standard bidding, you have a very normal response. With only 8 points and without three card support for partner's spade suit, you respond 1 NT.

What happens to your hand after the following rebids?

PTNR	OPP'T	YOU	OPP'T
1♠	Pass	1 NT	Pass
2♣, 2♦ or 2♥	Pass	?	

If partner's rebid was 2♣ or 2♦, your best rebid is 2♠. Partner's bids have shown at least nine cards in the two suits he mentioned. That leaves very little room for support in hearts. Occasionally a heart rebid will work out, but the odds greatly favor returning to partner's guaranteed five card spade suit.

However, if partner's rebid was 2♥, your hand suddenly

grows tremendously in value. Your 8 points now may be revalued to at least 11 points. Five cards in the trump suit plus your queen in partner's five card suit magnify the value of your hand.

A raise to 3 ♥ is clearly indicated. With a conservative partner even a jump to 4♥ is not out of line.

Here are how the three combined hands may look:

	PARTNER		PARTNER		PARTNER
1.	♠ A K 9 7 5	2.	♠ A K 9 7 5	3.	♠ A K 9 7 5
	♥ A 9		♥ 8 2		♥ K J 9 4
	♦ 8 2		♦ K J 9 4		♦ 8 2
	♣ K J 9 4		♣ A 9		♣ A 9
	YOU		YOU		YOU
	♠ Q 8		♠ Q 8		♠ Q 8
	♥ Q 10 6 5 3		♥ Q 10 6 5 3		♥ Q 10 6 5 3
	♦ A 6 5		♦ A 6 5		♦ A 6 5
	♣ 8 7 5		♣ 8 7 5		♣ 8 7 5

You can see how in Hands 1 and 2, where partner had bid clubs and diamonds, your safest spot was a part score spade contract. In Hand 3, with the "same point count," game becomes a very good bet when partner's rebid is in hearts.

So, as you make your bidding decisions at the table, keep in mind the fluidity of your values, *for better or for worse.*

THE CARE AND FEEDING OF THE TAKEOUT DOUBLE

The most used, misused and abused convention is the Takeout Double.

There are three aspects of the takeout double: the double, the response and the rebid. There are also three places where players go wrong: the double, the response, the rebid.

Since these are the areas where players tend to go wrong, let's address each of them.

The Double

First, we'll review briefly what most of us know about the takeout double.

What is the purpose of the bid? The opponents have opened the bidding in a suit and you would like to get into the action. The *ideal* double says:

"Partner, I need your help. I have at least opening bid strength and support for the unbid suits. Tell me which is your best suit. I'm asking you to bid even if you have *no points*."

Shape Is Everything

The ideal hand for the takeout double contains shortness in the opponent's suit and length and strength in the three other suits.

A good general rule is: The more your hand is distribution-ally ideal, the less high cards you need. The less ideal, the more points.

Unfortunately, you don't always get ideal hands. Before doubling, consider all of partner's possible responses. If you can't handle them adequately, don't double.

"I had to double. I had 14 points," one hears time and again. 'Taint necessarily so! If you cannot safely handle any response by partner, you have two alternatives.

1. *Pass.*

   Your hand may be better suited for defense. Also, your problem may be solved by your left-hand opponent's response. If the opening bid is passed around to your partner he may be in position to make a balancing bid. He might possibly double, overcall in a suit or bid notrump.

2. *Overcall.*

   Alternatively, with a good five card suit you can overcall. With a 16 point balanced hand you may be able to bid one notrump. Occasionally, with a good four card major suit, such as A K J 10 or A Q J 9, you might even overcall at the one level.

With what kind of "nonideal" hands can you make a takeout double?

Your right-hand opponent has opened the bidding with 1 ♦. You hold:

A.	B.	C.
♠ A Q 9 8	♠ A Q 8 6	♠ A K J 9 7 6
♥ A J 10	♥ A Q 9 3	♥ K Q 7
♦ 6 4 3	♦ 8 7 3	♦ 4 3
♣ K 9 2	♣ K 9	♣ A 10
BID: Double	BID: Double	BID: Double

A. You would like to have four hearts and one less diamond, but you don't. If partner responds in hearts or clubs, you plan to pass and play in a possible four-three fit.

B. You hold both majors and know that partner will strive to bid one of them. If he bids 2♣, you'll just have to live with it.

C. You're much too strong to make a simple overcall. Whichever suit partner responds in, other than spades, you'll now bid your spade suit independently. This shows a 17 point-plus hand and a very good suit.

The Response

In response to partner's takeout double, you know you have to bid *something*, even if you have *nothing*. This being the case, you have to differentiate between a poor hand where you're bidding from fright and a better hand where there's a prospect of game. With 9 or more points, you should by all means avoid responding in minimum terms.

EXAMPLES:		
Opener	Partner	Opponent	You
1 ♣	Double	Pass	?

A. ♠ J 10 6 3	B. ♠ Q J 10 8	C. ♠ A Q 8 7
♥ Q 4 2	♥ Q 10 4	♥ Q 10 8 7
♦ 6 3	♦ A 2	♦ A 2
♣ 10 8 6 3	♣ 10 8 6 3	♣ 8 6 3
BID: 1 ♠	BID: 2 ♠	BID: 2 ♣
D. ♠ A 3	E. ♠ 7 5 3	F. ♠ 7 5 3
♥ A Q J 9 8	♥ 9 8 7	♥ K 8 3
♦ K 3	♦ A 10 3	♦ A 10 2
♣ 9 8 6 3	♣ K J 9 2	♣ K J 9 2
BID: 2 ♣	BID: 1 NT	BID: 2 NT

A. You have no choice. With zero to 8 points, you respond in your best suit and at the lowest possible level.

B. You can't make the same response as on hand A. You have to show partner you have a reasonable hand, 9 to 11 points. The jump bid is descriptive but not forcing.

C. You have a 12 point-plus hand with both major suits. You want to be in game, but you shouldn't try to guess which suit to bid. Instead, cue bid the opponent's suit, clubs in this case, and throw the decision back to partner. The cue bid says nothing about your club holding; it merely indicates a game-going hand.

D. Here again you want to be in game. You could jump to 4 ♥, but if so you'd relinquish all slam possibilities. If you cue bid the opponent's suit, it will signal a very good hand and give you more leeway in exploring for slam.

E. Good stoppers in opponent's suit, no suit of your own but a moderately good hand, bid 1 NT (7 to 10 points).

F. Similar to hand E but a better hand; bid 2 NT (11 or 12 points).

The Rebid by the Doubler

Here is where you have to watch your step. Remember, when you doubled you forced your partner to make a bid even if he held zero points. So if partner makes a minimum response, and you have a minimum hand too, you simply pass. You might not be delighted with partner's response, but you still have to pass.

(If, with a minimum hand, you cannot stand partner's response, you probably didn't have a sound takeout double in the first place.)

A very common mistake is for the doubler to blithely go on bidding with a minimum hand. A forward going bid on your part indicates a 17 point-plus hand.

A jump rebid requires an even stronger hand, asking partner to go to game if his hand contains a smattering of valuable high cards or features.

If partner's response was a jump bid in a suit (9 to 11 points) or two notrump (11 to 12 points), the bid is descriptive and not forcing. You may pass with a real minimum, invite game with a medium hand and go directly to game with a good hand.

If you, with a good hand, do not know where to place the contract, you cue bid the opponent's suit, eliciting further information from partner. Likewise, if you have some slam aspirations, cue bidding is often the best solution.

EXAMPLES:

Opp't.	You	Opp't.	Ptnr.
1 ♦	Double	Pass	1 ♥, 1 ♠ or 2 ♣
Pass	?		

A. ♠ A Q 9 3 ♥ A Q 6 4 ♦ 4 3 ♣ J 6 3	B. ♠ A K 9 3 ♥ A Q 6 4 ♦ 4 3 ♣ K 6 3	C. ♠ A K 10 8 6 3 ♥ K 7 ♦ 8 7 4 ♣ A K

A. Regardless of which suit partner bid, you have no real choice, since your hand is minimum. You must pass.

B. Raise partner in spades or hearts, but pass if his response was 2♣. Partner can bid on in the major or pass, depending upon the strength and texture of his hand.

C. If partner bid a spade, raise him to 3♠. If partner bid 1♥, simply bid 1♠, showing a 17 point-plus hand and a good spade suit. Likewise, if partner responded 2♣, bid 2♠.

EXAMPLES:

Opp't.	You	Opp't.	Ptnr.
1 ♣	Double	Pass	2♦, 2♥, 2♠ or 2NT
Pass	?		

D. ♠ A J 10 8 ♥ A J 7 6 ♦ K 6 3 ♣ 6 3	E. ♠ A Q 10 7 ♥ A Q J 6 ♦ Q 8 6 ♣ 7 4	F. ♠ A J 10 7 ♥ K J 9 8 ♦ Q J 4 3 ♣ 9

Partner's jump response in a suit indicates 9 to 11 points. The 2 NT response indicates 11 to 12 points.

D. A pass is indicated in the four cases with this minimum hand.

E. Over 2♦, 2♥ or 2♠, a raise to three is appropriate. Over a 2 NT response, raise to three.

F. Over partner's jump response in diamonds, pass. Game in a minor suit is not likely. Likewise, over 2 NT, there just is not enough strength to continue. However, if partner bid 2♥ or 2♠, your shape might easily produce a game. A raise to three is very reasonable. Partner can pass with a minimum and go to game with a maximum.

WHAT IS A REVERSE BID?

I am sure you have heard the term "Reverse Bid" many times. But in my experience with many bridge-playing friends, the true significance and implications of the Reverse Bid are not fully understood.

Let's go to the *Official Encyclopedia of Bridge* for an authoritative definition of a Reverse Bid: "An unforced bid at the level of two or more in a higher ranking suit than that bid originally."

Here are some examples:

A. OPENER	RESPONDER	B. OPENER	RESPONDER
1 ♣	1 ♠	1 ♥	2 ♦
2 ♥		2 ♠	

C. OPENER	RESPONDER	D. OPENER	RESPONDER
1 ♦	1 NT	1 ♦	2 ♣
2 ♥		2 ♥ (or 2 ♠)	

In each of these auctions, responder cannot return to open-er's original suit without going to the *three level*. Don't you think you should have a *really strong* hand to force your partner to that level?

Most modern players regard a reverse bid as a one-round force. Therefore, in order to make such a bid the opener should have 17 or more points. If the opener has at least 17 points and the responder 6 or more, at least 23 points are indicated in the combined hands. Game possibilities are there-fore good, and it is advisable to keep the bidding going.

The great majority of experts play a reverse by the opening bidder as forcing for one round. Reverse bids by the responder are certainly forcing.

EXAMPLES:

A. OPENER	RESPONDER	B. OPENER	RESPONDER
1 ♦	1 ♥	1 ♦	2 ♣
2 ♣	2 ♠	2 ♦	2 ♥ (or 2 ♠)

In both cases, opener must go to the three level to return to responder's first bid suit, hence it is a reverse bid, and forcing. (In addition, still another new suit bid by responder is also forcing. Boy! Is that bid forcing!)

We should also look at auctions which are *not* considered reverses, so that we can recognize the differences when we come across them.

EXAMPLES:

A. OPENER	RESPONDER	B. OPENER	RESPONDER
1 ♦	1 ♥	1 ♣	1 ♦
1 ♠		1 ♥ (or 1 ♠)	

Auctions A and B are both at the *one level*, and responder can safely return to opener's original suit at the *two level*. Therefore neither of these rebids is considered a reverse bid.

All the examples above have assumed uncontested auc-tions. In contested auctions a different criterion applies. Here are a couple of examples:

C. OPENER	OPPONENT	RESPONDER	OPPONENT
1 ♦	2 ♣	2 ♥	Pass
2 ♠			

D. OPENER	OPPONENT	RESPONDER	OPPONENT
1 ♣	1 ♠	2 ♦	Pass
2 ♥			

Both auctions include an interference bid by the enemy, thus forcing responder into the two level. The opening bidder is forced to bid again (responder has bid a new suit) and is simply describing his hand. His bid is not in any sense a reverse. If there had been no opposing bidding, the response and opener's rebid would have been made at the one level.

Now that we have a general understanding of "Reverse Bids," PLEASE . . . PLEASE . . . PLEASE . . . don't do what I've seen so often:

You hold this hand:

♠ 10 2, ♥ A K 8 4, ♦ 8 7 5, ♣ A Q 9 8. And these two auctions take place:

	YOU	OPPONENT	PARTNER	OPPONENT
A.	1 ♣	PASS	1 ♠	PASS
	REBID: ?			
B.	1 ♣	PASS	1 NT	PASS
	REBID: ?			

Don't bid 2 ♥, and later after the debacle explain, ". . . But, partner, I wanted to show you I had a four card heart suit."

In both these auctions, you shouldn't want to play the hand in hearts unless partner can bid the suit on his own.

In example A, partner is unlikely to have four hearts. Rebid one notrump. (If partner does hold a hand containing five spades and four hearts, there is nothing to prevent *him* from bidding hearts on his next turn.)

In example B, partner has almost *guaranteed* he does not have four hearts. Just pass before the walls cave in.

Remember, a reverse bid is a *strength-showing* bid.

Knowing what we now do about reverse bids, let's see how we would bid these few hands.

1. ♠ Q 3	2. ♠ 7	3. ♠ 8 7
♥ K Q J 7	♥ K Q 8 6	♥ K J 6 4
♦ A K Q 9 8	♦ 8 5	♦ A 9 3
♣ 8 7	♣ A K J 9 6 3	♣ A Q 10 6
YOU PTNR.	YOU PTNR.	YOU PTNR.
1 ♦ 1 ♠	1 ♣ 1 ♠	1 ♣ 1 NT
Rebid: ?	Rebid: ?	Rebid: ?

4. ♠ 9	5. ♠ A K Q 8	6. ♠ 8 6
♥ A K 8 4	♥ A K J 8 7	♥ K 4
♦ A Q J 6 3	♦ 9 4	♦ A K Q 9
♣ 10 7 6	♣ 8 6	♣ A Q 10 9 8
YOU PTNR.	YOU PTNR.	YOU PTNR.
1 ♦ 1 NT	1 ♥ 2 ♣	1 ♣ 1 ♠
Rebid: ?	Rebid: ?	Rebid: ?

HAND 1. You hold a solid 17 point hand. You can therefore afford to "reverse." Bid 2♥. Partner has many options: (1) He can rebid a good five card spade suit. (2) With club strength he can bid two notrump or three clubs. (3) He can support hearts. (4) He can bid 3♦.

HAND 2. You're not strong enough to reverse. You have a good six card suit; simply rebid 2♣. If partner holds five spades and four hearts he can now bid two hearts with a strong enough hand.

HAND 3. Rebid: Pass. Your hand is balanced and game is virtually impossible. One notrump seems as good a contract as any.

HAND 4. Rebid: 2♦. With the opponents holding at least nine spades between them, notrump may prove to be a disaster. Partner has at least seven cards in the minors. Hopefully some of them are in diamonds.

HAND 5. Rebid: 2♠. You have 17 high-card points, and partner has 10 points for his two club bid. Game is highly likely. You've now described your hand correctly and partner is in good position to place the contract.

HAND 6. Rebid: 2♦. With 18 points you are surely strong enough to reverse. You are describing a hand with five clubs, four diamonds and at least 17 points. Let partner take it from there.

FAST ARRIVAL

FAST ARRIVAL VS. SLOW ARRIVAL

Fools rush in where angels fear to tread. He who hesitates is lost. Haste makes waste. Strike while the iron is hot. Look before you leap.

Is it any wonder that bridge players, too, are baffled by the conflicting alternatives: Should you leap quickly into contracts or should you proceed slowly? As with most advice in bridge, the answer is: "It all depends."

The opposing arguments are:

1. By proceeding slowly you will arrive at the most advantageous contract more often.
2. Your detailed bidding is too revealing to the defense. All too often, it gives them a blueprint to the killing defense.

Since we're generously dispensing axioms at this moment, let's try to sum it up this way:

A. *If you know where you want to be, up and bid it!*

B. *If where you should wind up is unclear, proceed slowly to obtain as much information as **possible**.*

A. FAST ARRIVAL

Partner opens with 1 NT (16–18 points) and you have a balanced hand with 17 points. Raise to 6 NT. Don't fool around with Gerber. If you bid 4♣, your left-hand opponent may double for a club lead, and that might be the only lead to set the hand.

FOR EXAMPLE:

North
♠ A 5 4
♥ K Q 6
♦ A J 9 3 2
♣ K 8

West
♠ J 10 9 8
♥ 10 7 2
♦ 8 6 4
♣ 6 5 2

East
♠ 6 3 2
♥ 9 4 3
♦ 7 5
♣ A Q 9 4 3

South
♠ K Q 7
♥ A J 8 5
♦ K Q 10
♣ J 10 7

If the bidding goes:

South	West	North	East
1 NT	Pass	6 NT	Pass
Pass	Pass		

the odds highly favor West leading the ♠jack, in which case South has twelve tricks right off the top.

However, if the bidding goes:

South	West	North	East
1 NT	Pass	4 ♣	Double
4 ♥	Pass	?	

North now has a number of alternatives, none of which is clear-cut:

1. Guess that a diamond slam is makable and bid 6 ♦.
2. Gamble to bid 6 NT (which goes down on a club lead).
3. Settle for 4 NT.

Surely, in this type of situation your best bet is to "up and bid it!"

B. SLOW ARRIVAL

You have opened with a 2♣ bid (strong and artificial). Partner now makes a positive response of 2♥. Don't go jumping to 4♥ or 4♠. Partner's positive response has already guaranteed game. You cannot be passed out below game. Proceed slowly at *low levels* and try to ascertain where you want to play the contract, whether in a suit or notrump, and also to determine if a slam is possible. Even a grand slam may be in the offing.

Give yourself bidding room with good hands of open-ended strength. Don't always go jumping into Blackwood. Unless the *number* of aces and kings is your *only* concern, cue bidding may be a better approach.

The texture and the fit of the combined hands are often a better clue to slam bidding than the number of aces.

GAMES TRIES

On borderline hands, how to try for game and still be able to stop in a part score if the hands don't mesh is a subtle art.

The typical circumstances where this occurs are:

YOU	PARTNER
1 ♠	2 ♠
?	
1 ♥	2 ♥
?	

You hold 16 to 18 points on a revalued basis, and would like to make a forward move toward game if partner has the right type of hand.

In our less sophisticated days, we would raise partner's 2♠ bid to 3♠, or the 2♥ bid to 3♥. This would advise partner: If you have the top of your bid, go to game; otherwise, pass.

But experience has shown that often it is not *how strong* you are, but *where* your strength lies, that counts.

The trend now is to use "help suit" game tries. That is, the opening bidder bids a new suit in which he has a number of losers. If the responder has either strength or shortness in that suit, and a decent hand, he jumps to game. Otherwise he returns to three of the original suit.

(It is important to remember that after you raise partner's opening bid, and he then bids a new suit, it is forcing for one round.)

EXAMPLES:			
PARTNER ♠ A K J 6 5 ♥ K Q ♦ 5 3 ♣ K 10 8 6	YOU (Hand A) ♠ Q 8 7 4 ♥ 7 5 4 ♦ Q 10 9 4 ♣ A 5	or	YOU (Hand B) ♠ Q 8 7 4 ♥ A 5 ♦ Q 10 9 4 ♣ 7 5 4
BIDDING:	PTNR. YOU 1 ♠ 2 ♠ 3 ♣ 4 ♠		PTNR. YOU 1 ♠ 2 ♠ 3 ♣ 3 ♠

After you raised partner's 1♠ to 2♠, he made a "help suit" game try by bidding 3♣. In Hand A, your ace-doubleton will help reduce partner's losers in the club suit. A jump to game is indicated. In Hand B, you have three club losers, the chances of making game are slim. Settle for a part score, bid 3♠. You will notice that the high-card points are the same in both hands. The help suit game try has helped you make the proper decision.

The old sequence of 1♥, 2♥, 3♥ (and 1♠, 2♠, 3♠) is now used more as a preemptive measure. It is used with distributional hands containing poor defensive values to make it difficult for the opponents to enter the bidding.

SLAM BIDDING

When the combined partnership holding contains 33 or more high-card points, slams are not difficult to arrive at successfully.

But when the point count is lower, the factors of distribution and fit come into play.

In slam bidding, *where* key cards are located is often more important than how many points or aces you hold.

This is particularly true when the most important asset of a hand is its distributional strength.

Let's take a look at this example:

You Hold:	Partner Holds Either:	
♠ A K Q 6 5 4	A. ♠ J 9 8 7	B. ♠ J 9 8 7
♥ A Q 6 5 4	♥ K 7	♥ 10 7
♦ K 5	♦ 8 7 6	♦ 8 7 6
♣ —	♣ 9 8 7 6	♣ K 9 8 7

Playing strong two bids, the bidding would go:

IN COMBINATION A:		IN COMBINATION B:	
You	**Partner**	**You**	**Partner**
2 ♠	2 NT	2 ♠	2 NT
3 ♥	4 ♠	3 ♥	3 ♠
5 ♣	5 ♥	4 ♥	4 ♠
6 ♠	PASS	PASS	

or if you play weak two bids, with 2♣ the strong bid:

IN COMBINATION A:		IN COMBINATION B:	
You	**Partner**	**You**	**Partner**
2 ♣	2 ♦	2 ♣	2 ♦
2 ♠	3 ♠	2 ♠	3 ♠
4 ♥	5 ♥	4 ♥	4 ♠
6 ♠	PASS	PASS	

Although you hold only 18 high-card points, just the most modest kind of a fit in either spades or hearts will give the partnership a game. This justifies a strong two bid.

Notice how partner's Hand A gets stronger with your rebid of hearts. The ♥king really pulls its full weight.

In Hand B, with the same high-card point count, the ♣king is of no benefit.

The complete hands:

HAND A.

North
- ♠ J 9 8 7
- ♥ K 7
- ♦ 8 7 6
- ♣ 9 8 7 6

West
- ♠ 10 3
- ♥ J 3
- ♦ A 10 9 3
- ♣ A J 5 4 2

East
- ♠ 2
- ♥ 10 9 8 2
- ♦ Q J 4 2
- ♣ K Q 10 3

South
- ♠ A K Q 6 5 4
- ♥ A Q 6 5 4
- ♦ K 5
- ♣ —

CONTRACT: Six spades by South
OPENING LEAD: ♠three.

A normal trump break and a four-two heart split are all that are necessary for the fulfillment of the small slam contract, even though the combined hands hold only 22 high-card points.

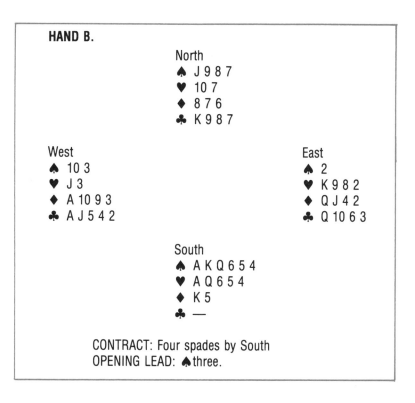

HAND B.

North
♠ J 9 8 7
♥ 10 7
♦ 8 7 6
♣ K 9 8 7

West
♠ 10 3
♥ J 3
♦ A 10 9 3
♣ A J 5 4 2

East
♠ 2
♥ K 9 8 2
♦ Q J 4 2
♣ Q 10 6 3

South
♠ A K Q 6 5 4
♥ A Q 6 5 4
♦ K 5
♣ —

CONTRACT: Four spades by South
OPENING LEAD: ♠ three.

You can see that a slam is not possible in this combination of cards, although the point count is the same as in the A version. Even with the heart finesse on, South still has to lose two diamond tricks.

To make a slam successful, the heart finesse has to be on and the suit has to break three-three. The partnership was wise to settle for a game contract.

When trying for slam with distributional hands, look for fits in side suits and the location of key cards. Blackwood is not the answer. Cue bidding is.

LISTEN AND LEARN

Throughout this book, in virtually every chapter—whether on defense, declarer play, bidding—you've read or heard these repeated cries: "If you listened to the bidding," "According to the bidding," "Review the bidding" or "Lack of bidding."

The reason is simple enough. Close attention to the bidding pays off in every aspect of the game. It helps greatly to reveal the opponents' or your partner's strength and/or distribution.

It acts as a guide to all facets of defense—especially opening leads. By the time it is your turn to lead, you often have garnered enough information to make the opening salvo much more than just a blind shot in the dark.

How do you listen? What are your thought processes as you hear bids and passes? Here is a simple example:

You are South, holding this hand: ♠ K J 9 5 ♥ A J 7 6 ♦ Q 3 2 ♣ 10 5. West, the dealer, bids one club and your partner passes.

You can guess that the opening bidder, playing Standard American, has at least three or four clubs and probably 13 or more points. *But what have you learned from partner's pass?* All he did was say one word, "Pass."

One thing you can be reasonably sure of is that partner does *not* have a good five card suit in diamonds, hearts or spades. The easiest way to enter the auction is to overcall at the one level (and over one club it can be done with a minimum amount of risk).

Your first assumption, therefore, is that partner has a poor hand with no good overcallable five card suit.

Other possibilities are: Partner may have a pretty fair hand with (a) a preponderance of strength and length in clubs, or (b) a balanced distribution unsuitable for a takeout double or a one notrump overcall.

Subsequent bidding developments may indicate which type of hand partner has.

If East now makes a positive bid, such as one spade, your first assumption is very likely correct. In any event, you pass and await further clarification of the opponents' bidding.

If East passes, however, it is good bet that partner has one of the second category of hands. You are now in position to make a balancing double.

If the bidding proceeds "pass," "pass," you know that partner has lots of clubs. Any other bid by partner would tend to indicate the more balanced type of hand.

The reason I'm bringing up this particular bidding sequence as an example is to stress the importance of getting inferences from the opponents' and partner's *passes*, as well as from their bids.

SAME WAVELENGTH AS PARTNER

A regular partnership has many practical as well as subtle advantages.

Your bidding system jells better. You are aware of partner's defensive habits. You know whether partner responds to legitimate defensive signals—attitude, count and suit-preference. If you know partner reacts to them, you use the signals. If not, you don't, since you'll be helping the declarer more than the partnership.

The subtle advantages include such things as knowing whether partner is basically conservative or aggressive.

Sitting down with a new partner is something else again. Most of us play "Standard American." But what Standard American is to one person is not necessarily what it is to another. Therefore, a couple of minutes of discussion is in order.

Usually, I opt to play whatever *reasonable* system the "stranger" wants to play . . . and the simpler, the better.

The fewer "new" things partner has to contend with, the fewer mistakes and misunderstandings will occur. When trying to cope with new approaches, partner often winds up not doing the good things he or she customarily does.

What basic things do you want to settle? Do you usually open four-card majors or do you require five-card major suit opening bids?

Limit or forcing jump raises? Weak two bids or strong two bids? If weak two bids, what is the forcing response?

And what does the rebid mean? Feature? If partner is accustomed to "feature" responses, don't try to teach him "Ogust."

If you've ever played in an individual tournament, you are aware that you wind up playing with a new partner every two hands. That gives you about thirty seconds to discuss your methods.

The best approach is strong two bids, forcing jump responses, Stayman and Blackwood, PERIOD!

How about Gerber? If they insist, but then only over opening one or two notrump bids.

Some people say, "Only when obvious." However, what is obvious to one person is not necessarily obvious to another.

SHARPEN YOUR GAME WITH
DUPLICATE BRIDGE

I recommend duplicate bridge if you want to sharpen up your game.

It's probably true that many social bridge players are simply afraid to play duplicate bridge. When I'm lecturing or directing bridge games on cruise ships, I frequently run into this syndrome.

But tell me this. How would you like to play a game holding terrible cards all evening long, and still *win*?

Duplicate bridge is about the only game that gives you this opportunity.

You might be the world's finest player, but if you hold poor cards in a rubber bridge game, *forget it . . . you won't win.*

On cruises, I urge many players who never played duplicate before to try it. After a few hands they get the hang of the mechanics, and from then on it's smooth sailing.

How can duplicate bridge improve your game?

First, you're able to compare what you accomplished on a particular hand with what everyone else did on the very same hand. In duplicate bridge your results are compared with what others have done with the same "crummy" or excellent hands, as the case may be.

With a little postgame analysis, you will recognize some of the errors you might have made and improve your technique if and when similar situations arise again.

And you'll feel real good when others have stopped at a

game contract, and you and your partner have bid and made a cold slam!

In rubber bridge, if you bid four in a major and make five, you might pat yourself on the back and go blithely on to the next deal. But what you might not realize is that you should have been in *six*, and with proper play would have made it.

For learning the mechanics and basic concepts of duplicate, a free booklet, "Easy Guide to Duplicate Bridge," is available from the ACBL (American Contract Bridge League, 2200 Democrat Road, Memphis, Tennessee 38116).

When you first start duplicate bridge, simply try to play good solid bridge and then later you will get into the more subtle strategies of the game.

By good solid bridge, I mean bid all the makable games, but settle for part scores on the more tenuous hands. Defend hands up to the hilt. That's where you can gain lots of points. Hold the opponents to one trick less than the other defenders do, and you pick up all the marbles.

At the outset, don't try to do anything unusual or fancy. You don't have to be perfect to win in duplicate bridge! A 65 percent result will usually win most duplicate bridge games.

If you'd like to play duplicate bridge, check with your local ACBL bridge club. Most clubs have "novice" games. These are games where all participants have fewer than 20 master points.

Many churches, synagogues, Elks clubs and Y's also have regular games where the competition is generally on a moderate as well as social level. Coffee and refreshments are often served and a pleasant afternoon or evening is available for a nominal fee. Most clubs accommodate singles and try to match you up with a compatible partner.

What is the main difference between rubber bridge and match-point duplicate?

In duplicate bridge it is not by *how large a score* you win on a particular hand, but by *how many pairs* you beat that determines your standing.

The *frequency* of gain is important, not the *amount* of gain.

To fully understand this concept, let us look at two similar circumstances.

Case 1. You have bid three notrump, not vulnerable, and made ten tricks. You receive a score of 430 points. All the other pairs playing the same hand bid and made four spades, scoring 420 points. You would receive the top score.

Case 2. Here again all the *other* pairs bid and made four spades, scoring 420 points. But this time, at your table, your vulnerable opponents decided to get into the bidding. You doubled and defeated them four tricks for 1100 points! You would receive the top score.

In Case 1, the difference between your results and the other pairs was only 10 points. *In Case 2*, the difference was 680 points . . . *but in each case you receive the same number of match points—a top score.*

Strategies in Duplicate Bridge

With small differences being so important in match-point duplicate, the competition for part scores is often spirited.

In competing for part scores, the three level is often the magical plateau.

If your side holds the higher ranking suit it is often wise to compete to this plateau . . . provided you can do so with reasonable safety. Reasonable safety means avoiding a 200 or 300 point set.

Whose Hand Is It?

The key to winning part-score tactics is to figure out "Whose hand is it?"

If your side has the preponderance of strength (Example: your partner opened the bidding and you hold 10 high-card points), this is considered "your hand."

You have competed to the three level, but the opponents have outbid you because they have a higher ranking suit. You got up to three hearts and the opponents bid three spades.

You feel you can make three hearts, but game is unlikely. What do you do at this point?

For bidding and making three hearts you would earn 140 points (90 points for three hearts plus a 50 point part-score bonus). You don't want to bid anymore because you feel you cannot make four hearts and you don't want to wind up with a minus score. So the best you can hope for is to defeat the opponents.

But just defeating them may not be enough. Setting the opponents one trick vulnerable or even two tricks nonvulnerable will give you only 100 points. In either case it is less than the 140 points you could have made for fulfilling your three heart contract.

Your best action, if you have a reasonable chance to beat three spades, is to *double the opponents* and hope for a 200 or 300 point set. Sometimes you even get a bonanza and earn a 500 point set.

Of course, once in a while, the distribution is such that the opponents make their contract and they wind up with a game bonus and a big score. What you get for your efforts is a big, fat zero!

But what have you really lost? If it was *your* hand, and the opponents made 140 undoubled, you were heading for a bad score anyway. You traded a one or a two match-point score for a zero this one time. But three or more other times, by doubling, you may go from a low score to a top score.

Now let's look at the other side of the equation, where the shoe is on the other foot. The opponents have the preponderance of the strength, not you. This is *their* hand.

Your best tactic is to push them up as *high* as you safely can. When you are not vulnerable you can be more aggressive. If you can hold your contract to a one-trick set, you are headed for a reasonable score. Even if the opponents double you, the loss is only 100 points, which is less than their making a part score at the three level.

If the opponents have reached the three level and your hand is not suitable for another bid, let them play it *undoubled.*

Remember, this is *their* hand. Defend against it the best you can. If they make their contract, you will obtain a normal result. If you hold them to one trick less than the other defenders, you will get a very good score. If you defeat them, you will probably get an excellent score. So don't double them.

The part score tactics simply stated are:

If it is *your* hand, and you have reached your limit, and the opponents bid on, *double them* if you think they're overboard.

If it is *their* hand, push them up as high as you safely can, then let them play it *undoubled . . .* and defend it to the hilt.

IMPORTANT CONVENTIONS

There are a number of conventions and treatments that on the whole are more effective in duplicate bridge than in rubber bridge. At the top of the list are the Weak Two Bids and the Negative Double.

THE "WEAK" TWO BID IS TWO WEAPONS IN ONE BID ... WHEN USED PROPERLY.

...HOWEVER, IT SURE CAN BACKFIRE, WHEN IT'S NOT!

THE WEAK TWO BID

The Weak Two Bid is an effective tool if used properly. It is both preemptive and descriptive. It announces a hand of less than opening bid high-card strength which contains a six card suit.

It is a limit bid showing 6 to 11 points, as most players use it. To be most effective as a preemptive bid, most of the points should be in the suit bid.

A weak two bid can be made in diamonds, hearts or spades. The opening two club bid is reserved as an artificial device to describe a very strong hand.

What is a Good "Weak" Two Bid?

Always remember the dual purpose of a weak two bid: It is preemptive as well as descriptive.

As a preemptive bid, its aim is to eat up some of the opponents' bidding room. A 2♠ opening bid is therefore the most effective weak two bid. The opponents will often have to compete at the three level or higher in order to get into the action.

Here are two hands, each with 10 high-card points and a six card suit.

1. ♠ A Q J 9 8 6   ♥ 10   ♦ K 7 3   ♣ 10 5 3
2. ♠ J 8 7 6 5 3   ♥ A Q 10   ♦ K 10 9   ♣ 3

In hand no. 1, most of your strength is in your long suit. With six cards in the spade suit a second trick might not survive, defensively, without being ruffed. The opponents might be able to make four hearts, the other major, and yet find it difficult to enter the auction. Even if the opponents obtain the contract, you'd be delighted to get a spade lead from your partner.

The preemptive benefits in this hand are quite clear, and the texture of the hand is fully descriptive of a weak two bid.

In hand no. 2, let us first examine its preemptive values. You wouldn't object seriously if the opponents were to get into a heart or a diamond contract. All your high cards are in these suits. Even against a club contract you have excellent defense assets in your *short suits*.

Also, you wouldn't be particularly happy if partner were to lead a spade against an opponent's contract.

Hand no. 1 is an excellent weak two bid. Bid 2♠.

Hand no. 2 is a poor weak two bid. The proper bid is "Pass."

Position Is Everything in Life

Does the position you're in make a difference when you're thinking of opening a weak two bid?

The position is often quite critical.

In first and second position, you are not only preempting your opponents, you may also be preempting your partner. Partner may be the one with the good hand.

When opening a weak two bid in first or second position, therefore, your hand should be as close to the ideal as possible. A six card suit with "good texture" is usually essential. Some players even promise they have two of the top three honors.

If your long suit is diamonds, I would recommend you *guarantee* two of the top three honors. This enables your partner to bid a notrump game with one of the top honors and an appropriate holding in the other three suits.

Another good policy to follow in first or second seat is: Don't open a weak two bid in a major if you hold four cards in the other major. Here again, you may be preempting your partner. Besides, you have potentially good defense if the opponents arrive at a contract in the other major.

In third position is where you can be the most flexible. Your partner has already passed and you, therefore, can't very well have a game. Your side most likely does not even have the preponderance of the high-card strength. Making it difficult for the opponents to get into the act may prove very effective.

In some cases, experienced players will open weak two bids in third seat holding only five cards in the suit.

The use of an opening two bid in *fourth seat* is an entirely different matter. The need for preempting has mostly disappeared. If you have a poor hand, and you think the opponents are more likely to make a plus score, you have a very simple remedy. You just pass.

A few other factors have to be considered. In high-card strength you should be near the top of the two bid range. If your six-bagger is in diamonds, it is best to forget it. The opponents can usually outbid you in one of the majors.

The spade suit is your best bet for a two bid, since you hold the highest ranking suit. If your long suit is hearts, the hand should contain some good defensive prospects in case the opponents wind up in a spade contract.

Remember, when you open in fourth position your goal is to wind up with a *plus score*. Even a game may be possible if partner has exactly the right cards. The weak two bid is not just a defensive bid, it is primarily an *offensive* bid. In fourth seat, therefore, a "weak" two bid is really a fairly strong bid.

How Vulnerable Are You?

Vulnerability plays a big role in deciding whether or not to bid a weak two.

Let us consider the various possibilities.

1. UNEQUAL VULNERABILITIES
   (a) You are vulnerable; they are not.
   (b) They are vulnerable; you are not.

   (a) *Unfavorable Vulnerability.*
        (You:Vul. vs. They:Nonvul.)
        This is the worst time for a weak two bid. You cannot
        afford to go down more than *one* trick, if doubled.
        Anything more than that would present the oppo-
        nents with at least 500 points, which is greater than
        the 400 to 460 points they might make in a game
        contract.
           You therefore should have a very substantial suit
        with top high-card values to justify such a weak two
        bid. Partner should be able to count on you for this
        type of hand if and when he responds to your two
        bid. He also can make better defensive judgments,
        based on this assumption.
   (b) *Favorable Vulnerability.*
        (You:Nonvul. vs. They:Vul.)
        This is the most favorable time for a defensive weak
        two bid. You may go down three, doubled, and still
        lose fewer points to the opponents if they have a
        vulnerable game. A 500-point set, as against a vul-
        nerable game of 600-plus points.
           Your weak two bids, (particularly in third seat) can
        be really free-wheeling when the vulnerability is fa-
        vorable.

2. EQUAL VULNERABILITY
   (a) Both sides Vulnerable.
   (b) Both sides Nonvulnerable.

   (a) *With each side vulnerable*, the weak two bidder can
        afford to sustain a two-trick doubled set of 500 points
        as against a vulnerable game of 600-plus points for
        the opponents.
           Your vulnerable two bids should be prudent. Solid

in first and second position, a bit more flexible in third position.

Maybe the best way to describe your attitude with both vulnerable is that you should make standard weak two bids. After all, your opponents are vulnerable too. They may be hesitant to compete against you, afraid of winding up with a big penalty.

(b) *With both sides not vulnerable*, standard considerations should also apply here. It is true that the weak two bidder can sustain a two-trick doubled set of 300 points as against a 400-plus nonvulnerable game for the opponents. But being nonvulnerable, the opposition is less fearful about getting into the act.

With equal vulnerability, therefore, the best way to play the weak two bids is down the middle . . . "Play it like it's writ!"

Responses to Partner's Opening Weak Two Bid

Once you decide to incorporate weak two bids in your game, a method of partnership communication becomes necessary.

How do you react after partner has opened a weak two bid? Based upon your holding, you first have to decide whether *game is likely or unlikely*.

If game is unlikely, you have a couple of tactics at your command.

1. **PASS.**

   If you have a hand containing good defensive features, it is not a bad idea to let the opponents get into the bidding. You may have a good chance to set their contract. Even doubling the opponents is a possibility if they get too high.

2. **CONTINUE THE PREEMPT.**

   You simply raise partner's suit to the three or four level. Hands in which you have good trump support for partner but poor defense against opponents' possible contracts qualify for this type of bid. Vulnerability must be taken into consideration, so that you don't go too far overboard. The general idea is to preempt as high as you can safely do so. Even a jump raise of partner's 2♦ bid to 5♦ (or 6♦) is appropriate in some instances.

If game is a good possibility, there are a number of methods and conventions that are available.

1. If you "know" you want to be in game and also know the right contract, *just up and bid it.*

   Partner opened 2♥ or 2♠. Bid 4♥ or 4♠. Partner opened 2♦. Bid 3 NT or 5♦. The advantages of going right to game are twofold. First, the auction is unrevealing to the opponents. There is no guide to their defense. Secondly, in suit contracts, they don't know whether you're preempting with a bad hand or raising with a good hand.

2. If you need further clarification from partner, the standard procedure is to respond with a forcing 2 NT bid.

   This asks partner to describe his hand. There are two popular methods of rebids in answering the forcing 2 NT bid. Feature and Ogust. Let's explain the simpler one first.

Feature

The 2 NT bid asks the opener to rebid a side suit in which he holds a "feature," an ace or a king. If he doesn't have a feature he simply rebids his original suit.

EXAMPLES:			
Opener	Partner	Opener	Partner
2 ♠	2 NT	2 ♠	2 NT
3 ♦ (I hold the ♦A or ♦K)		3 ♠ (I have no feature)	

One additional possibility exists. If the opener has a solid, "runnable" suit: A K Q X X X, he rebids 3 NT.

Based on opener's rebid, the 2 NT bidder is now in a position to place the final contract, whether three or four of a major suit or three notrump.

Ogust

The Ogust convention is more complex, but quite thorough. Partner gets a very good picture of opener's hand.

The system is based upon step responses, in answer to partner's forcing 2 NT bid.

REBID: 3 ♣ = Poor hand. Poor suit.
3 ♦ = Poor hand. Good suit.
3 ♥ = Good hand. Poor suit.
3 ♠ = Good hand. Good suit.
3 NT = A K Q X X X in original bid suit.

EXAMPLES:			
	YOU OPENED 2 ♥ REBID: ?		PARTNER 2 NT
Hand A. ♠ K 6 REBID: 3 ♣	♥ K J 9 6 5 3	♦ 9 6 3	♣ 6 4
Hand B. ♠ 9 3 REBID: 3 ♦	♥ A K 10 8 7 6	♦ 10 6 2	♣ 6 4
Hand C. ♠ A 6 REBID: 3 ♥	♥ K J 8 6 4 2	♦ Q 6 5	♣ 8 2
Hand D. ♠ K 9 REBID: 3 ♠	♥ A K 10 9 7 6	♦ J 7 6	♣ 7 6
Hand E. ♠ 9 3 REBID: 3 NT	♥ A K Q 7 6 2	♦ 9 6 3	♣ J 3

Based upon your rebid, the 2 NT bidder can place the contract. Partner can even explore for slam with the appropriate hand.

In addition to 2 NT as a forcing bid in response to opening weak two bids, some people play a new suit bid by an unpassed hand as forcing. (Some players don't. They play 2 NT as the only force.) Agree with your partner on which way to play.

If you decide to play a new suit as forcing, your rebid is dependent upon your holding in partner's new suit and your holdings in the other unbid suits.

EXAMPLES:	
YOU OPENED 2 ♥ REBID: ?	PARTNER 2 ♠ (Forcing)

Hand A. ♠ K 6	♥ A K 10 6 5 4	♦ 8 6 5	♣ 8 7
REBID: 3 ♠			
Hand B. ♠ 9 3	♥ A J 10 7 6 3	♦ Q 10 8	♣ Q 9
REBID: 2 NT			
Hand C. ♠ 8 5	♥ A Q J 8 6 5	♦ 9 3 2	♣ Q 5
REBID: 3 ♥			

Under this method:

A. You should support partner's suit with as little as two cards to an ace, king or queen.
B. With no support for partner's suit, rebid 2 NT with a hand containing face cards in the unbid suits.
C. Otherwise, simply rebid your suit.

THE STRONG TWO CLUB OPENING BID

With 2♠, 2♥ and 2♦ no longer available as strong opening bids, the catchall 2♣ opening bid is used in all cases where a strong two bid is appropriate, regardless of which suit the hand contains as the prime suit.

Responses to the artificial strong 2♣ bid are handled much the same way as responding to the natural strong two bids. The prime exception is that the *negative* response to 2♣ is 2♦. This describes a hand of less than seven high-card points. A response of 2 NT, therefore, is a *positive* bid describing a hand of seven or more points with no biddable five card major suit.

When the responder makes a negative reply, (2♦) the opening bidder then describes his hand. He bids his suit or notrump as the hand may dictate.

While some regard an opening 2♣ bid as game forcing, an increasing number of people play it as forcing to two no-trump or to three of a major suit. This gives the partnership greater flexibility and is in keeping with the modern practice of opening two notrump bids in the range of 20 to 22 points.

When the opening 2♣ bidder has a balanced hand, these auctions may take place after a negative response of 2♦:

	Opener 2 ♣	Responder 2 ♦		Opener 2 ♣	Responder 2 ♦
REBID: (A)	2 NT		REBID: (B)	3 NT	

The following auctions may take place when the opening 2♣ bid was based on a hand with a suit:

	Opener 2 ♣	Responder 2 ♦		Opener 2 ♣	Responder 2 ♦
REBID: (C)	2 ♥ or 2 ♠		REBID: (D)	3 ♣ or 3 ♦	

A. Opener's rebid of 2 NT indicates a balanced hand of 23 or 24 high-card points (a hand too strong to have opened 2 NT). Responder may now pass with 0–2 points. With 3 or more points, responder has a few options: Bid 3 NT; Bid three of a five card suit or bid four of a six card major suit. (Bid 3♣ Stayman, or use Jacoby transfers by partnership agreement.)

B. Opener's 3 NT rebid indicates a balanced hand of 25-plus points. Responder will usually pass, but with freakish distribution he may bid his suit. With a balanced 5 or 6 point hand, responder may try for slam with a quantitative 4 NT bid. (This would not be Blackwood.)

C. Responder must bid again. The 2♥ or 2♠ bid is forcing. Responder now describes his hand naturally.

D. The 3♣ or 3♦ bid is natural and forcing. Responder must bid again, describing his hand as well as he can.

THE NEGATIVE DOUBLE

The Negative Double convention is used when your partner has opened the bidding (1♣, 1♦, 1♥ or 1♠) and your right-hand opponent has overcalled in another suit, thereby interfering with your normal response.

At this point you say "Double." This tells partner, "I would have been able to make a bid if the opponent had not over-called." The negative double is basically a takeout double. It asks partner to bid.

When the opponent's overcall is in a major suit, your negative double strongly suggests you have the other major.

Here are a few examples:

PARTNER 1 ♣	OPPONENT 1 ♠	YOU ?
You hold:		
A. ♠ 9 6 3 ♥ K J 8 5 ♦ 10 9 6 3 ♣ A 9 BID: Double	B. ♠ J 7 ♥ A J 9 8 ♦ K Q 6 4 ♣ 10 9 3 BID: Double	C. ♠ 9 8 6 ♥ K J 8 7 5 ♦ A 10 5 ♣ 6 4 BID: Double

A. This is a minimum type hand. You would have bid 1 ♥ had the opponents not overcalled. The negative double indicates you have values that are hard to describe with any other bid.

B. You have a good 11 point hand, but only four hearts. A 2 ♥ bid would guarantee a five card suit. The negative double provides the best way to tell your story.

C. You have a five card heart suit, but only 8 high-card points. 2 ♥ would be a gross overbid. The negative double frequently overcomes the dilemma where you can't afford to pass and can't afford to bid.

PARTNER 1 ♦	OPPONENT 2 ♣	YOU ?
You hold:		
D. ♠ 8 7 5 ♥ K Q 9 6 ♦ K J 8 3 ♣ 10 9 BID: Double	E. ♠ 8 6 ♥ K Q 10 8 7 ♦ A J 6 ♣ 9 8 6 BID: 2 ♥	F. ♠ 9 6 3 ♥ A 9 2 ♦ 10 8 ♣ K Q 10 9 6 BID: Pass

D. You would like to tell partner you have a four card major. Double. If partner bids 2 ♠ you can safely retreat to 3 ♦.

E. You have a good five card heart suit and 10 high-card points. You show them by simply bidding 2 ♥.

F. If you play negative doubles, you can't double at this point for penalties. You pass and hope partner will reopen with a balancing double, in which case you plan to pass and thus convert partner's balancing double into a penalty double.

When you have room to bid a major suit at the one level, the call you choose will depend on whether the opponents overcalled in a major or a minor suit.

PARTNER 1 ♦	OPPONENT 1 ♥	YOU ?
You hold:		
G. ♠ K J 9 7 ♥ 10 8 7 ♦ 9 8 6 ♣ A 5 4 BID: Double	H. ♠ K J 9 7 3 ♥ 8 7 ♦ 9 8 6 ♣ A 5 4 BID: 1 ♠	

When the opponents overcall in hearts, you have room to bid spades at the one level. To show a *four card* spade suit (Hand G) you double. To show a *five card* spade suit (Hand H) you bid 1 ♠.

PARTNER 1 ♣	OPPONENT 1 ♦	YOU ?
You hold:		
I. ♠ 10 7 2 ♥ K J 9 7 ♦ 9 3 2 ♣ A J 4 BID: 1 ♥	J. ♠ K J 9 7 ♥ 9 3 2 ♦ 10 7 2 ♣ A J 4 BID: 1 ♠	K. ♠ K J 6 3 ♥ Q 10 7 2 ♦ 9 3 ♣ K 6 4 BID: Double

When the opponents overcall one club with one diamond, you may bid a four card major suit (Hands I and J). A double would indicate four cards in *both* majors (Hand K).

PTNR.	OPP'T	YOU	PTNR.	OPP'T	YOU
1 ♥	1 ♠	?	1 ♠	2 ♥	?

You hold:	You hold:
L. ♠ 8 6	M. ♠ 8 7
♥ 9 2	♥ 9 4
♦ Q J 10 8 7	♦ A J 8 6
♣ K Q 8 6	♣ K Q 10 6 2
BID: Double	BID: Double

When one major is overcalled by another, a double suggests support for both minor suits (Hands L and M).

REBIDS BY THE OPENING BIDDER

Let's return now to the opening bidder. Rebids by the opener have to take into consideration partner's action after the opponents overcalled.

1. *Partner made a negative double.*

   Opener should bid a new suit, if feasible, especially the unbid major suggested by partner's double. Opener bids on the minimal level with up to 15 point hands, jumps with 16 to 18 points (nonforcing and invitational) and cue bids the opponent's suit with 19 or more points.

   With appropriate hands containing good stoppers in the opponent's suit, opener may bid notrump at various levels depending upon the strength of his hand.

   Occasionally, opener may *pass*, converting partner's negative double into a penalty double. This generally requires a strong holding in the opponent's suit and shortness in partner's presumed suit.

2. *Partner passed.*

   The opening bidder should reopen with a balancing double whenever it is reasonable to do so. Partner, with length and strength in the opponent's suit, may have been forced to pass previously. In that case, he may now pass again, converting the balancing double into a penalty double.

3. *Partner bid a suit.*

Partner's suit bid (forcing) and his *failure to use the negative double* supply valuable information to the opening bidder. Here are some examples:

A. YOU	OPPT.	PARTNER
1 ♦	1 ♠	2 ♥

You know partner has at least five hearts and at least 10 points.

B. YOU	OPPT.	PARTNER
1 ♣	1 ♥	1 ♠

Partner has at least five spades. If he had only four, he presumably would have doubled.

C. YOU	OPPT.	PARTNER
1 ♣	1 ♦	1 ♥ or 1 ♠

If partner bids 1 ♥ or 1 ♠ you know he doesn't have the other major. With both majors he presumably would have doubled.

D. YOU	OPPT.	PARTNER
1 ♥	1 ♠	2 ♣ or 2 ♦

You can feel reasonably sure partner does not hold *both* minor suits. With both minors, he presumably would have doubled.

So when partner bids a suit over the opponent's overcall, opener bids naturally, taking full advantage of the subtle inferences available to him.

Rebids by the Negative Doubler

Opener generally clarifies his holding by his rebid. If opener makes a minimum response, showing 12 to 15 points, and you have a minimum too, it is usually wise to pass. With 11 or 12 points invite game. With 13 or more points, go directly to game or cue bid the opponent's suit.

TRANSFER BIDS

The principle of permitting the strong hand to become declarer in a suit contract is the chief basis for the use of transfer bids.

Transfer bids are used when partner has made an opening bid of one or two notrump (or even three notrump, if it is a natural bid).

Jacoby transfer bids are used at the two and three levels. Texas transfers are used at the four level.

Jacoby Transfer Bids

Jacoby transfer bids permit the opening notrump bidder to become the declarer in a major suit.

The basic process is simple. After partner's opening one notrump bid, you, as responder, holding a major suit of five or more cards, bid 2♦ if your suit is hearts, bid 2♥ if your suit is spades. Partner is obligated to respond in the next higher ranking suit. After an opening two notrump bid the process is the same, except it is one level higher.

EXAMPLES:

1.	PTNR.	YOU	2.	PTNR.	YOU	3.	PTNR.	YOU
	1 NT	2 ♦		1 NT	2 ♥		2 NT	3 ♦
	2 ♥			2 ♠			3 ♥	

Transfer bids can be used with good hands, poor hands or mediocre hands. Your subsequent rebid will describe to partner which type you hold.

EXAMPLES:

Partner has opened 1 NT. You hold:

A.	♠ J 9 8 7 5 3		B.	♠ K 9		C.	♠ K J 10 8 7 6	
	♥ J 5			♥ K 10 9 8 3			♥ 9 7	
	♦ 10 3			♦ 8 7			♦ K 10 3	
	♣ 9 7 6			♣ Q 10 6 2			♣ 8 2	
	PTNR.	YOU		PTNR.	YOU		PTNR.	YOU
	1 NT	2 ♥		1 NT	2 ♦		1 NT	2 ♥
	2 ♠	Pass		2 ♥	2 NT		2 ♠	3 ♠
D.	♠ K Q 10 8 7		E.	♠ A 7		F.	♠ K Q 10 9 3	
	♥ K 9			♥ A K 10 9 6			♥ A 9	
	♦ Q 10 6 2			♦ 9 2			♦ A J 3	
	♣ 8 7			♣ K 10 7 6			♣ J 10 4	
	PTNR.	YOU		PTNR.	YOU		PTNR.	YOU
	1 NT	2 ♥		1 NT	2 ♦		1 NT	2 ♥
	2 ♠	3 NT		2 ♥	3 ♣		2 ♠	4 NT

A. With this poor hand, you would like it played in 2 ♠. Simply pass. You have made the strong hand declarer at what is almost surely the best contract.

B. You have accomplished the first step with your transfer bid. If the hand is to be played in hearts, the notrumper will be declarer. However, with this "in between" type hand you don't know what the final contract should be. Your 2 NT rebid describes your hand and gives partner a number of options.

With a minimum hand and a doubleton heart, partner passes. With three hearts partner may bid three hearts or pass; with four hearts he simply bids three hearts.

With a maximum hand (17-plus points) and a doubleton heart, partner bids 3 NT. With three or four card heart support partner bids 4 ♥.

C. Your 3 ♠ bid is invitational. It denotes a six card suit with a hand of moderate strength. Based upon partner's holding he may pass or correct to 3 NT or 4 ♠.

D. You have a game-going hand and your 3 NT bid says you belong in a game contract. Partner's options are to pass, or with three or four card spade support to take it to 4 ♠.

E. If partner has the right type of hand, slam is a possibility. You indicate that and the distribution of your hand by bidding a four card minor suit. You've now described your hand, and partner should be able to take it from there.

F. Here you have a truly strong hand. Slam is a good possibility. 4 NT is a quantitative bid indicating a balanced hand and a desire for slam if partner has a maximum. Partner, with a minimum, either passes or bids 5 ♠. With a maximum, he bids 6 ♠ or 6 NT.

Looking at the hand from the opening notrumper's point of view, he has no option but to reply to responder's transfer request, no matter how poor his holding is in the suit. However, if he has an exceptional hand with four card support he may jump in the indicated suit. This has two advantages. Responder may carry on to a makable game on a hand he might have otherwise passed. Or with a good hand, slam may be possible. Of course, with a truly horrendous hand responder may still pass.

EXAMPLES:

1.				2.				3.			
♠ A Q 6				♠ A Q 6				♠ K Q 10 2			
♥ 7 6				♥ K 7 6				♥ A 9			
♦ K Q 10 4				♦ K J 10 3				♦ A 10 9 4			
♣ A J 9 8				♣ A 6 4				♣ A 7 6			
YOU	PTNR.			YOU	PTNR.			YOU	PTNR.		
1 NT	2 ♦			1 NT	2 ♦			1 NT	2 ♥		
2 ♥				2 ♥				3 ♠			

1. You have no choice. You are not crazy about hearts, but you must bid 2♥ in response to partner's transfer bid.
2. This time you're happier with partner's transfer bid, but your bid is still the same, 2♥.
3. The value of your hand has suddenly jumped to about 20 points, and you should emphatically pass this good news along to partner by making a jump response to the transfer bid. Bid 3♠.

All the hands shown thus far contained only *one* major suit. With hands containing *two* major suits, Jacoby transfers are used *only* when *both suits are at least five cards long.*

The Stayman convention is used when one of the majors is a four card suit.

Here are the basics of handling major two-suiters after partner's opening notrump bid.

A.		B.		C.	
♠ K J 8 7 5		♠ K J 8 7		♠ K 10 9 3	
♥ Q 9 7 6		♥ Q J 7 6 5		♥ K Q 8 7 5	
♦ Q 5		♦ 8 5		♦ 7 6	
♣ 8 7		♣ J 4		♣ Q 4	
PTNR.	YOU	PTNR.	YOU	PTNR.	YOU
1 NT	2 ♣	1 NT	2 ♣	1 NT	2 ♣
2 ♦	2 ♠	2 ♦	2 ♥	2 ♦	3 ♥

In the above three examples, you have two major suits but one of them contains only four cards. Therefore, you use

Stayman. If partner denies having a major suit, you then bid your five card suit. You bid at the two level with a moderate hand, jump to three with a game-going hand. One advantage of using the Jacoby transfer system is that by your failure to employ Jacoby in this instance, your partner knows that you hold five-four in the majors.

D. ♠ Q J 9 8 6		E. ♠ K J 10 8 7		F. ♠ A K 10 8 3	
♥ K 10 8 7 5		♥ K Q 8 6 5		♥ K Q 9 6 4	
♦ 4		♦ 9		♦ 8	
♣ 6 5		♣ 8 7		♠ 8 6	
PTNR.	YOU	PTNR.	YOU	PTNR.	YOU
1 NT	2 ♦	1 NT	2 ♥	1 NT	2 ♥
2 ♥	2 ♠	2 ♠	3 ♥	2 ♠	3 ♥

When you transfer to one major suit and then bid the other major suit, you indicate at least five-five in the majors. The order in which you bid them indicates the strength of the hand.

With minimum hands which might not be of game-going proportions, transfer to hearts first and then bid spades.

In Hand D, you had bid 2 ♦ transferring to 2 ♥. You now bid 2 ♠. Partner knows by the sequence of your bids that you hold a minimum hand. Partner has these options: He may pass 2 ♠, or give a preference by bidding 3 ♥. A 3 ♠ bid would be invitational. With appropriate fits, he may jump to game in 4 ♥ or 4 ♠.

In Hands E and F, you have at least game-going strength. You show that by transferring first to spades and then bidding 3 ♥. Hand F has definite slam potential. After partner gives suit preference, probe for slam.

To sum up Jacoby transfers holding two five-card majors:
1. *With minimum hands*, bid 2 ♦ (transfer to 2 ♥) and then rebid 2 ♠.
2. *With good hands*, bid 2 ♥ (transfer to 2 ♠) and then rebid 3 ♥.

Texas Transfer Bids

Texas transfers are used at the four level. Jacoby transfers are at the two and three levels. They can be used independently of each other. However, you have the best of both worlds when you combine them into one system.

Texas transfers are used when you hold a major suit of six or more cards and partner has opened with a notrump bid.

You bid 4 ♦ as a transfer to 4 ♥. You bid 4 ♥ as a transfer to 4 ♠.

Here's how it works:

1. ♠ K Q 10 8 6 3		2. ♠ 6		3. ♠ 9 6	
♥ 10		♥ K J 9 7 6 4		♥ Q J 10 8 7 6 3	
♦ 8 5		♦ Q J 6 3		♦ Q J 3	
♣ Q 10 7 6		♣ 8 2		♣ 6	
PTNR.	YOU	PTNR.	YOU	PTNR.	YOU
1 NT	4 ♥	1 NT	4 ♦	1 NT	4 ♦
4 ♠	Pass	4 ♥	Pass	4 ♥	Pass

When Texas is used in conjunction with Jacoby transfers, you have an additional dimension in handling six-plus card suits.

When you first bid Jacoby transfer and then jump to four, you are showing a six card suit and slam potential. When you bid Texas, you are not interested in slam and are attempting to preempt the opponents.

EXAMPLES:

4. ♠ A K 8 7 6 4	5. ♠ A 9	6. ♠ Q J 10 8 6 4 2
♥ K 10 4	♥ K Q 10 9 7 6	♥ 7
♦ 9	♦ 8 3	♦ 10 9
♠ Q J 7	♣ K J 8	♠ K 4 3
PTNR. YOU	PTNR. YOU	PTNR. YOU
1 NT 2 ♥	1 NT 2 ♦	1 NT 4 ♥
2 ♠ 4 ♠	2 ♥ 4 ♥	4 ♠ Pass

In Hands 4 and 5, partner knows you are interested in slam. He can continue toward that goal with an appropriate fit and strength.

In Hand 6, you have signaled that you have no interest in slam by using the Texas transfer. The opponents may have a good save in the heart suit but you've robbed them of precious bidding space. They'd have to start experimenting at the five level.

Interference

When playing Jacoby transfers, the transfer is *off* when there is intervening bidding. You just bid in the same manner as if there were no transfer bids.

With Texas transfers, however, you have more room. If the interference is at three clubs (or below) you can still jump to 4♦ or 4♥ as transfers to 4♥ and 4♠.

EXAMPLES:

	PARTNER	OPPONENT	YOU
A.	1 NT	2 ♦	2 ♥
B.	1 NT	2 ♦	4 ♦
C.	1 NT	3 ♦	4 ♥

A. Your 2♥ bid is natural (and not forcing). Jacoby transfers are off after opponents' interference.

B. Opponents' interference is at or below 3♣. Your 4♦ bid is a Texas transfer to 4♥.

C. Opponent's interference is above 3♣. Your 4♥ bid is natural.

THE ONE-HOUR-A-WEEK ROAD TO BRIDGE SUCCESS

I am sure many of you have asked yourselves, "How can I improve my game?"

How about trying my "For Cryin' Out Loud," one-hour-a-week practice session. I'm sure you'll have fun and make giant improvements in your bridge game at the same time.

Most of us, playing social bridge, play for about two to three hours. Once a week, with your favorite partner and group, allocate the first hour to our "little practice game." Then use the balance of the time for your regular play.

Here's how it works: The key to the method is thinking "out loud." In doing this, each bid and play made is reacted to orally by the players. You might be surprised by how much you can learn about the hand, thus making the bidding and play clearer and easier.

A practice round of four hands gives each player an equal opportunity to participate and should be completed in about one hour.

Cut for dealer and start as you would normally. After the hand is dealt, the person to the *right* of the dealer is designated as *the caller.* Just to keep things straight we'll call him "Righty."

Righty simply explains what each bid and play of the other three players meant to him. After Righty bids, the dealer explains what Righty's action meant to him.

Let's go through a couple of typical hands to see how our script plays.

Bidding

DEALER			"RIGHTY"
South	West	North	East
(1) 1 ♠	(2) Pass	(3) 1 NT	(4) Pass
(5) 2 ♥	(6) Pass	(7) 3 ♥	(8) Pass
(9) 4 ♥	(10) Pass	(11) Pass	(12) Pass

RIGHTY: (1) "Dealer has at least five spades and, most likely, 13 or more points.

(2) "West has no reason to bid at this time.

(3) "North has 6 to 9 points and most likely less than three spades in his hand."

DEALER: (4) "Righty has no good reason to bid at this time. I know very little about his point count."

RIGHTY: (5) "Dealer has at least four hearts. That indicates he has at least nine cards in the major suits.

(6) "West has no reason to bid at this time.

(7) "North has at least four hearts and probably 8 or 9 high-card points. His hand most likely revalues to about 10 points."

DEALER: (8) "Righty still has no bid at this time."

RIGHTY: (9) "Dealer's hand revalues to 16 or more points."

(10-11-12) No comments are necessary on these passes, which make West the opening leader.

At this point the scene shifts to the opening leader who does his thinking aloud:

OPENING LEADER: (looking at the following hand)

♠ K J 10 4   ♥ 8 7   ♦ J 8 7 5   ♣ A 9 8

"Declarer, with at least nine cards in the majors, must have shortness in the minor suits. Dummy has shortness in the spade suit. The way I can best utilize my strong spades is by cutting down dummy's opportunity to trump them. To prevent what may be a crossruff, my best lead is a trump."

The ♥ eight is led and the dummy is exposed.

Declarer now has his turn at bat, and does his planning out loud.

THE DECLARER: (looking at his hand and dummy)

DUMMY
♠ 7
♥ A 9 4 2
♦ 9 6 4
♣ K J 6 4 3

DECLARER
♠ A Q 9 6 3
♥ K Q 10 5
♦ A 3 2
♣ 5

"The opening lead has reduced some of my ruffing ability. Let's see how many tricks I have for sure. One spade, four hearts and one diamond. That gives me six tricks. If the ace of clubs is on side, I'll have seven. I'll need three more tricks via ruffs. But if they continue with trump leads, perhaps my spade queen or club jack will set up as a trick.

"So I'll let the lead come around to my hand and then lead a club toward the dummy."

RIGHTY: (looking at his hand and dummy as declarer plays the ♥ two on the ♥ eight)

DUMMY
♠ 7
♥ A 9 4 2
♦ 9 6 4
♣ K J 6 4 3

                              EAST (RIGHTY)
                              ♠ 8 5 2
                              ♥ J 6 3
                              ♦ K Q 10
                              ♣ Q 10 7 2

"After seeing dummy's singleton spade, I'm glad partner led a trump. I'll just play my ♥ six; the jack might come in handy later."

Declarer wins the trick with the ♥ ten and leads ♣ five. West plays the ♣ ace, dummy the ♣ three.

RIGHTY: "I'll play the ♣ seven, starting a high-low to show partner I hold an even number of cards in the club suit."

West now leads the ♥ seven.

RIGHTY: "Partner is continuing the strategy of reducing the ruffing possibilities for declarer. I'll just play the ♥ three. I now know South started with four hearts."

Declarer wins the heart with the queen, then plays the ace of spades and ruffs a spade in dummy. When the declarer discards a small diamond on the ♣ king . . .

RIGHTY: "I now know declarer's original distribution: five spades, four hearts, one club and therefore three diamonds. Incidentally, I also know partner's distribution: four spades, two hearts, four diamonds and three clubs."

DECLARER: "I'll ruff a small club and hope the queen will drop. Then I'll be able to enter dummy with a trump lead and wind up with ten tricks."

Well, the queen doesn't fall. When a second spade is ruffed in dummy and the king doesn't fall, the declarer goes down one trick.

I suggest you play every hand "duplicate" style, where each player retains each card as he plays it. As a result, when the play is completed, you have the opportunity to see all four hands in the open, and discuss the bidding and play.

Let's look at the complete hand on the next page.

```
                        DUMMY
                        ♠ 7
                        ♥ A 9 4 2
                        ♦ 9 6 4
                        ♣ K J 6 4 3

        WEST                                    EAST
        ♠ K J 10 4                              ♠ 8 5 2
        ♠ 8 7                                   ♥ J 6 3
        ♦ J 8 7 5                               ♦ K Q 10
        ♣ A 9 8                                 ♣ Q 10 7 2

                        DECLARER
                        ♠ A Q 9 6 3
                        ♥ K Q 10 5
                        ♦ A 3 2
                        ♣ 5
```

In the hand just completed, an alternate line of declarer play is possible, and perhaps has a better percentage chance of success.

At trick three, instead of winning the trump lead in declarer's hand, he wins it in dummy, and takes the spade finesse (a 50 percent chance).

If it wins, a small spade is ruffed in dummy and the king of clubs is cashed, declarer discarding a diamond. A club is now ruffed and a low spade is next ruffed in dummy. Declarer enters his hand with the ♦ ace, draws the last trump and surrenders a diamond at the end, making eleven tricks.

However, since the ♠ king is offside, the contract cannot be made with the defense offered.

Please note how effective the opening trump lead was as well as the trump continuation at trick three.

So what have we learned from our first practice hand?

Did you (as Righty) notice how "easy" it is to count the hand, if you listen carefully to the bidding and watch the play of the cards? Did you feel any power surge when you figured out declarer's exact distribution?

The importance of the opening lead cannot be overstressed.

Close attention to the bidding will often provide the clue to the most effective opening lead and defense.

Declarer play can often take different routes. The successful route is not always easy to find. Playing with a plan, however, always essential. It doesn't always win, as the luck of the cards may not be with you on a given hand, but over the long haul, it will surely help you to come out on top.

After four hands have been played in the practice session, each person has had a chance to be the caller. Each time it was the player to the right of the dealer.

To vary the pace of our "For Cryin' Out Loud" sessions, we can alternate the procedure as to who "voices" the thoughts.

The one-caller-per-hand method can be used one week. Another method would be for *each individual* to describe the action taken by the previous player. For example, take an auction such as the following:

South	West	North	East
1 ♥	Pass	1 ♠	Pass
2 NT	Pass	3 NT	Double
Pass	Pass	Pass	

The dialogue would go something like this:

SOUTH: "One heart."

WEST: "South has a five card heart suit and about 13 or more points.
"Pass."

NORTH: "West has no reason to bid at this point.
"One spade."

EAST: "North holds at least four spades and at least 6 points.
"Pass."

SOUTH: "East has no reason to bid.
"Two notrump."

WEST: "South has 19 or 20 points and fewer than four spades.
"Pass."

NORTH: "Evidently West has no reason to bid.
"Three notrump."

EAST: "North believes they can make game.
"Double."

SOUTH: "East thinks he can defeat the contract if partner leads a spade. The double of a notrump contract asks his partner to lead the first suit bid by dummy.
"Pass."

WEST: "South believes he should stay put.
"Pass."

NORTH: "I guess West had no choice but to pass. The fat is in the fire . . .
"Pass."

This gives you an idea of how the alternate method of "calling" works. You can use one system one week, another system the second week. Or you can stay with the method that suits you best.

Oh yes! I suppose you'd like to see how this second hand came out.

West dutifully led the ♠ six.

Here is the complete hand:

```
                      North
                      ♠ A 8 7 5
                      ♥ 6 5
                      ♦ Q J 7 4
                      ♣ 8 6 4

West                                    East
♠ 6 3                                   ♠ K Q J 10 4
♥ 10 9 7 2                              ♥ A 3
♦ 10 9 8                                ♦ 5 3 2
♣ A 10 9 5                              ♣ 7 3 2

                      South
                      ♠ 9 2
                      ♥ K Q J 8 4
                      ♦ A K 6
                      ♣ K Q J
```

As can readily be seen, with the opening spade lead South cannot make the three notrump contract. In fact, a two-trick set is the final result.

Notice that any other opening lead permits declarer to make his contract.

If South had decided to pull out of the 3 NT contract and had tried a bid of 4♥, that contract, too, would have been defeated.

Most of us have heard of books where you're asked to look over the expert's shoulder as he bids and plays various hands of bridge. It's like "Sing along with Mitch."

Well, in our *practical* practice sessions, it's a case of "Think along with Thelma," . . . or whatever your names happen to be. Your friends will think along with you, and you with them.

First you think aloud in your practice sessions, and then to yourselves as the thinking patterns become part of your bridge habits. As you continue your practice sessions, many things you thought were difficult and even beyond your reach will fall into place and become understandable.

Such things as determining opponents' and partner's distribution, counting the hand, and card reading will be within your grasp. The methods that lead to effective opening leads and good defense will gradually become yours.

Realizing the power of distribution for game and slam bidding and avoiding getting too high on misfit hands are concepts that you will become aware of.

But equally important, your practice sessions will bring you added enjoyment and fun.

INSTANT REPLAY

As a guide to what has gone before, I am including this Instant Replay section which is a capsulization of significant areas that are part of *The Fun Way to Serious Bridge*.

You may want to refer to *The Fun Way to Serious Bridge*, or to this section, as a refresher to combine the basics of that book with the additional material in *The Fun Way to Advanced Bridge*. The book includes the following major areas:

Mechanics of the Game
Evaluating the Hand
    The Point Count System
    The Principle of the Average Hand

What is an Opening Bid?
  The Opening Bid of One in a Suit

Which Suit to Open

Goals of Bidding
How much *Combined* Strengh You Usually Need to Reach the Goals
  of Game and Slams
Responses to an Opening Bid of One in a Suit

6–9 points

10–12 points

Rebids by the Opening Bidder
1. When Responder has made a
    Minimum Limit Bid

Up to 15 points
*Settle for a
Part Score*

16 to 18 points
Invite Game

19 to 22 points
Go for game!

2. When Responder has made a
    Game-Forcing Limit Bid

3. When Responder has made an
   Unlimited Bid

Notrump Bidding
One Notrump Opening Bid

Responses to An Opening One Notrump Bid:
   With a Balanced Hand
   With an Unbalanced Hand
The Stayman Convention
Stayman Interference

Stayman =
Cue Bid in Opponent's Suit

Forcing Bids

Competition

Reasons for Competing
Ways of Competing
Simple Overcall
1. *Trick-taking ability* more important than points.
2. Would you be happy if partner led that suit in defense?
Responses to Partner's Overcall
1. Treat partner's overcall approximately as you would an opening bid, just be a trifle stronger on a single raise.
2. Notrump response is not a denial. It is a positive response, with good controls in opponent's suit.

Single Jump Overcall*

"Intermediate" jump overcall: good suit, 15–17 points.

* (Alternate approach: "Preemptive single-jump overcall.")

Direct One Notrump Overcall

Same as opening one notrump bid, with controls in opponent's suit.

Takeout Double

Responses to Partner's Takeout Double

Defense Against Takeout Double

"Redouble" indicates ten or more high card points. All other responses indicate less.

Cue Bid

A cue bid in opponent's suit is a super takeout double in Standard American practice.

Preemptive Overcalls

Used to upset flow of information between the opponents. Indicates a long suit, usually seven or more cards, with high-card strength within suit rather than outside it.

Unusual Notrump

Two notrump overcall describes a hand containing two minor suits of at least five cards each.

Big Hand Bidding

Strong opening bid of two in a suit is forcing.*

Opener should have twenty-plus points and be within one trick of game in own hand

* (When using weak two bids, two clubs becomes the strong forcing opening bid.)

Blackwood Convention

When *Not* to Use Blackwood

1. Avoid initiating Blackwood with hand containing a void.
2. When you have to know *which* ace partner has, not *how many*.
3. If negative response brings you above your trump suit level.

How to Play a Hand in Five Notrump after using Blackwood

Bid a new suit at the five level, which requires partner to bid five notrump.

How to Show a Void over Partner's Blackwood Bid

Indicate *useful* void by jumping to six level in the suit which shows how many aces you hold.

Grand Slam Force

When Blackwood is not used, a five notrump bid requests partner to go to seven in the agreed suit with two of the top three honors, or bid six with fewer.

Big Notrump Hands
　　Two notrump opening: 22 to 24 high-card points, balanced hand.
　　Three notrump opening: 25 to 27 high-card points. (Standard American practice)

Gerber Over Notrump
　　Four Clubs ace-asking bid.

Preemptive Opening Bids
　　Long suit, usually seven or more cards, below opening bid strength. Good suit, poor defensive strength.

Defenses Against Preemptive Bids
　　Takeout doubles, cue bids over three bids. Doubles over four bids primarily for penalties, four notrump for takeout.

Penalty Doubles

Patterns of Play

How to Win Tricks
　　1. High Cards　2. Long Suits　3. Ruffing

> A FINESSE IS AN ATTEMPT TO WIN TRICKS WITH *LOWER CARDS* BY TAKING ADVANTAGE OF THE FAVORABLE LOCATION OF *HIGHER CARDS* HELD BY THE OPPONENTS

Finesses
　　Simple Finesses
　　Double Finesses
　　Ruffing Finesses

GET ME OUT OF THE WAY, *FIRST!*

Establishing Suits

Usually, play high cards *first* from the hand containing the fewer cards

Give a Little To Gain a Lot

Declarer Play in Trump Contracts

Think Before Playing to First Trick
(The next trick may be too late)

1. HOW MANY LOSERS DO I HAVE? 2. HOW CAN I GET RID OF THEM?

When to Pull Trumps Immediately
    A. Don't need dummy's trumps for ruffing.
    B. Prevent opponents from ruffing side suit winners.
    C. You have sufficient trumps to maintain control of trumps.

When to Delay Pulling Trumps
    A. Dummy is short in a side suit.
    B. Hand can play as a crossruff.
    C. You need to discard losers before relinquishing lead
        in trump suit.
    D. You need dummy's trumps as entries.

Declarer Play in Notrump Contracts
Think Before Playing to First Trick

HOW MANY WINNERS DO I HAVE "OFF THE TOP"? IS THERE A DANGEROUS OPPONENT?

The Hold-Up Play
Keeping Dangerous Defender Out of the Lead

SAFETY
SAM

DANGEROUS
DAN

Which Suit Do I Set Up?
1. Which suit provides all the tricks you need.
2. Which suit gives you greatest safety.
3. Which suit gives you alternate choices.

Maintaining Lines of Communication
1. Entries in a side suit.
2. Entries within the suit.

Defensive Play
Opening Leads
Notrump Leads
Which card to lead:
Blind Leads: Top of sequence; top of interior sequence; fourth
best.
Leading Partner's Bid or Implied Suit:
Headed by a single honor or nontouching honors, lead lowest
from three or four cards (or fourth-best card).
Headed by two touching honors, lead top honor.
With small cards, lead lowest from four cards; lead highest from
three cards; lead highest from any two cards.

Rule of Eleven
If player has led "fourth best" in a suit, you subtract that card from
11. This will tell you how many cards *higher* than the card led
there are outside the leader's hand.

Opening Leads Against Suit Contracts
Which card to lead:
Top of touching honors; fourth best from single or nontouching

honors; low card from three cards headed by an honor. (Do *not* underlead aces.)

Top from any two-card holding; lead king from ace-king when suit contains at least three cards.

Lead of ace followed by king shows a doubleton.

Avoid leading from tenace combinations: AQJ, AJ10, KJ10, unless it is partner's bid suit.

Third Hand Play

With touching honors or a sequence, third hand plays the bottom of the sequence.

Unblocking: With a doubleton headed by an honor, unblock, by playing your honor when partner leads top of a sequence.

Signals

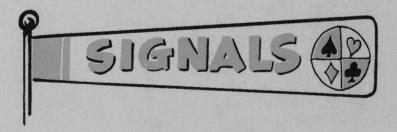

ATTITUDE: High-Low = Continue
           Low-High = Discontinue
COUNT: High-Low = Even number of cards in suit.
       Low-High = Odd number of cards in suit.

SUIT PREFERENCE: To indicate a preference between two suits, signal in a third suit. High card for the higher ranking suit, low card for the lower ranking suit.

HOW DO I LET HIM KNOW I PREFER DIAMONDS?

Lead Directing Doubles
Double of a notrump contract:
A double by the partner of the opening leader directs him to:

1. Lead a suit bid by the defending side.
2. If no suit was bid by the defending side, lead the first suit bid by dummy.

Double of a freely bid slam contract:

1. Lead the first suit bid by dummy (other than the trump suit).
2. If no suit has been bid by dummy, make some other unusual lead.
3. In no case lead a suit bid by the defending side.

Double of a conventional bid or cue bid directs opening leader to lead that suit.

Advanced Play
The Strip and End Play
The Simple Squeeze
Dummy Reversals
Deceptive Play, Falsecarding
Your Bridge System
Proprieties and Pleasures
Playing in the Real World of Bridge
This is an abbreviated description of some of the conventions, treatments, methods and systems in current use. The purpose of this section is to acquaint the reader with a general knowledge of these procedures. The reader can adopt some of these methods to his own use or can be in better position to cope with these actions when confronted with them in actual play.
The Weak Two Bid and Responses
Preemptive Single-Jump Overcalls
DOPI Convention
Method of coping with opponent's interference over your Blackwood or Gerber ace-asking bid.

THE SMARTEST
CONVENTIONAL BID
IS DOPI

The Delicate Art of Balancing

Third (and Fourth) Hand Openings

Drury (over Partner's third or fourth hand major suit opening bid)

Negative Double

Transfer Bids

Flannery

    Two diamond opening bid shows five hearts and four spades with 11 to 15 points. Two no trump forcing response. Rebids show distribution and/or strength.

Big Club Systems

FLANNERY WILL GET YOU EVERYWHERE...

...IF YOU HOLD FIVE HEARTS AND FOUR SPADES!